BRUCE TEMPLETON

Strictly Confidential

*Dancefloor Drama, Sparkle Showdowns & the Secrets
Behind the Sequins*

This book was professionally typeset on Reedsy.
Find out more at reedsy.com

Contents

1

About the Author

Bruce Templeton is a lifelong lover of ballroom, a former professional dancer turned choreographer and teacher, and an unapologetic *Strictly Come Dancing* superfan. He took his first dance steps in patent leather shoes at the age of six and never looked back - touring internationally as a Latin and ballroom champion throughout the late 1990s before swapping the spotlight for the studio.

These days, Bruce runs a boutique dance school in Sussex, where he teaches everything from Viennese waltzes to wedding first dances (with an emphasis on flair). He's known for his signature foxtrot, fondness for feathered costumes, fierce loyalty to the *Strictly* glitterball - and for being routinely upstaged by his two sausage dogs, **Fred and Ginger**, who never miss a results show.

When he's not teaching a tango or rewatching the iconic Jay

McGuiness jive, Bruce writes passionately about dance, pop culture, and the shows that bring sparkle to our screens. *Strictly Confidential* is his unabashed love letter to the sequins, sweat, and sheer joy of Britain's best-loved show.

2

From the Glitterball, With Love

I t starts with a drumbeat. A flash of lights. A shimmer of
sequins. And then, like clockwork, the music kicks in and
you're swept away - not just by the dancing, but by the
drama, the glamour, the journey. If you're anything like me -
and if you've picked up this book, I suspect you might be - that
opening number on a Saturday night does something special to
your soul. It's not just a TV show. It's *Strictly Come Dancing*.

I remember watching the very first episode in 2004 with a glass
of Merlot in one hand and a velvet cushion clenched nervously
in the other. I had spent years on the professional dance circuit,
waltzing in and out of competitions, training rooms, and the
kind of dressing rooms where sequins outnumbered safety pins
ten to one. I'd hung up my Latin heels by then - mostly - but
when *Strictly* arrived on our screens, it was as if the ballroom
had come home. Suddenly, the nation cared about the cha-cha.
Teenagers were talking about the tango. My neighbour asked
me what a fleckerl was. A *fleckerl*, for heaven's sake!

That was when I knew: this show had legs - and not just the beautiful ones high-kicking across the floor.

Over the years, *Strictly* has become more than just a competition. It's a celebration. A tradition. A glitter-soaked spectacle that invites the famous, the forgotten, and the frankly rhythm-impaired to take a leap into something terrifying and trans-formational. We've cheered for underdogs, wept over surprise exits, shouted at the judges (well, *one* judge in particular - no names, but we all know who), and held our collective breath during those cruel, cruel dance-offs.

In this book, I'm throwing open the stage door and taking you behind the velvet curtain - not to tear down the magic, but to show you just how much love, sweat, and sparkle goes into making it. We'll revisit the early days and the late-night rehearsals, the wardrobe dramas and the live show miracles. We'll talk icons and underdogs, heartbreaks and historic wins. And yes, we'll dig into the glitterball gossip too - because darling, it wouldn't be *Strictly Confidential* without a bit of shine and shade.

You'll also meet some of my personal favourites - not just the headline-makers and trophy-lifters, but the ones who left their hearts on the floor, even if their feet weren't quite sure what they were doing. Because in the world of *Strictly*, progress often means more than perfection.

Writing this book has been a joy, a jive, and occasionally a full-blown dramatic paso doble. I've laughed, cried, rewatched *that* Alexandra Burke samba four times in a row, and even enlisted the help of my two faithful sausage dogs, Fred and Ginger, who've offered their unfiltered opinions from the sofa (Fred prefers Halloween Week, Ginger is partial to the Charleston).

So whether you're a die-hard fan or just someone who knows the difference between a rumba and a roast potato (though just barely), I hope this book makes you fall in love with *Strictly* all over again - or maybe even for the first time.

One final note before we begin: *Strictly Come Dancing* has always been a show about more than dancing. It's about transformation. Courage. Connection. And, above all, joy. That joy is contagious - and you, dear reader, are part of it.

Now... places, everyone.

The glitterball awaits.

Much Love

Bruce

x

3

Born to Dance

From Come Dancing to Strictly

I t's hard to imagine now, in an age where *Strictly Come Dancing* is practically part of the British constitution, but there was once a time when ballroom dancing was considered old-fashioned, dusty, and better left in faded Blackpool postcards than on primetime television. But before the glitterball gleamed and before Bruce Forsyth's voice welcomed us with that unmistakable twinkle, the seeds of the *Strictly* phenomenon were already nestled deep in British broadcasting soil - in a little show called *Come Dancing*.

I was barely out of primary school when I first heard the orchestral swell that introduced *Come Dancing*. My mum - a rock'n'roll lover with a secret passion for a good foxtrot - used to set her knitting down and watch with quiet reverence. To her, *Come Dancing* wasn't just a show; it was proof that grace, style, and sequins still had a place on screen. I didn't know it then, but those Saturday nights planted the first sparkle of obsession in me. Fast forward a few decades, and I'd be dancing for a living. But let's not get ahead of ourselves.

The origins of *Come Dancing* date back to 1949, making it one of the BBC's longest-running and most beloved light entertainment programmes. It wasn't exactly the edge-of-your-seat viewing we expect today - no voting public, no backstage meltdowns, and certainly no samba rolls in sight - but it had its charm. Teams from different regions competed in various ballroom and Latin styles, all judged with the poise and precision of a genteel village fête. It was very proper. Very polite. And yet, it held an almost hypnotic rhythm, a grace that spoke to a Britain still brushing off the soot of wartime and yearning for elegance.

For years, *Come Dancing* gently sashayed along, peaking in the 50s and 60s when ballroom was booming across the country. Every town had its own dance hall. Every bride and groom knew at least a basic quickstep. Dance wasn't just entertainment - it was social survival. But as pop culture exploded, and new forms of music and movement swept in, the show gradually fell out of fashion. By the late 80s, it was something your nan watched with a cup of Horlicks. Still respectable, but no longer relevant.

The final *Come Dancing* broadcast aired in 1998. And for a while, that seemed to be that. Ballroom dancing slipped into the background, cherished by diehards and studio devotees, but largely ignored by the wider public. Even I had stepped away from the competitive floor by then, having worn through my third pair of Latin heels and developed an aversion to feathers.

I was teaching by that point - wedding dances, social cha-chas, corporate team-building tangos (yes, really) - and wondering if the golden age of ballroom had well and truly passed.

But television, like dance, is cyclical. It reinvents, reframes, and - when it's feeling brave - resurrects.

Behind the scenes at the BBC, a handful of producers were quietly dreaming up a concept that would bring ballroom back, but with a twist. What if the formality of *Come Dancing* was combined with the emotional tug of reality TV? What if everyday celebrities - actors, newsreaders, sports stars - were partnered with professional dancers and trained to perform live each week? What if audiences could vote? What if ballroom was given not just a facelift, but a full-blown makeover in glitter and spotlight?

The concept was risky. Dance, at that point, was seen as niche. Too posh. Too technical. Too... well, not *fun*. But executive producer Richard Hopkins and entertainment legend Fenia Vardanis believed otherwise. With the right blend of nostalgia and novelty, they knew ballroom could sparkle again. The format was loosely inspired by *Come Dancing*, yes - but this would be something entirely different. Faster, funnier, fiercer. And crucially, more emotional. They wanted the nation to *feel* something.

The next big challenge was the title. Early drafts floated ideas like *Celebrity Dance-Off* and *Star Steps* (neither of which, thank goodness, made it past the brainstorm stage). Eventually, someone suggested a clever play on the Baz Luhrmann film *Strictly Ballroom*, and the rest, as they say, was history. *Strictly Come Dancing* was born - a name that both honoured the past and winked cheekily at the present.

When the show was finally greenlit, there were nerves. Television executives weren't sure whether viewers would tune in, whether celebrities would say yes, whether the nation would care. But there was one thing everyone agreed on: if *Strictly*was going to work, it needed the right host. And who better than the master himself - Bruce Forsyth.

Bruce brought instant credibility and warmth. A veteran of entertainment, his presence grounded the show in familiarity, even as its format sparkled with innovation. Paired with the ever-graceful Tess Daly, the two became the face of a new Saturday night ritual. I remember watching that first broadcast with a strange mix of hope and trepidation - would this work? Could ballroom be cool again?

The first series premiered in May 2004. It was, in some ways, a modest start. Only eight celebrity contestants. A simple studio. Judges seated at what looked suspiciously like a repurposed cabaret bar. But the heart was there. The dancing was earnest, the stakes were clear, and the chemistry - between celebs and pros, judges and audience - crackled with potential. Natasha Kaplinsky and Brendan Cole emerged as early favourites, their chemistry electric, their performances slick. But more importantly, viewers *cared*. People were talking about samba rolls over the watercooler. My neighbour - the same one who once asked about fleckerls - now had strong opinions about Viennese hold.

The format was a hit, and the BBC knew it. Viewing figures climbed steadily. Word-of-mouth buzzed. Critics who had scoffed at the idea of foxtrots on primetime were suddenly writing think-pieces about the return of elegance. And behind it all was that strange, wonderful magic: the joy of watching someone grow.

Because that's the thing about *Strictly* - it's not just about dance. It's about transformation. The shy ones who find confidence. The stiff ones who find rhythm. The cynical ones who fall in love with the process. And we, the audience, go on that journey with them. Week after week, step by step, tear by triumphant tear.

So while *Come Dancing* laid the foundation, *Strictly Come Dancing* took that history and gave it hips. It honoured the past while dancing joyfully into the future - sequins and all.

And the rest? Well, that's what this book is for.

Next, we meet the people who dared to put their reputations - and their ankles - on the line for our entertainment. The celebrities. The cannon-fodder. The surprise finalists. The scandal-makers. The stars in their eyes... and dancing shoes.

Casting the First Series

If you think teaching the cha-cha to a stubborn hedge fund manager is difficult, try convincing a panel of celebrities to dance it on live TV. In tight trousers. With the nation watching. The truth is, casting the first series of *Strictly Come Dancing* was less like assembling a light entertainment lineup and more like matchmaking in a fever dream - part charm offensive, part calculated chaos. The BBC knew they needed recognisable names, of course, but they also needed the right mix: a soap star, a news anchor, a sports hero, a wildcard. Too famous, and they'd be too careful. Too obscure, and nobody would vote. The sweet spot was somewhere between *Hello!* magazine and the post office queue.

Back in early 2004, the casting department set to work on what would become one of the most unpredictable lineups in British television history. Their brief? Find eight celebrities brave (or bonkers) enough to learn ballroom dancing from scratch, rehearse six days a week, and perform live on Saturday nights - in sequins. And make sure they don't all say no.

To their credit, they cast their net wide. Early conversations included pop singers, presenters, TV chefs, ex-athletes, and the odd MP. Some were flattered, others bewildered. A few declined outright - one actress reportedly said she wouldn't "humiliate herself by dancing with a stranger on the BBC." I'd bet money she regrets that now.

But a few were curious. And from that curiosity bloomed a cast that felt, at the time, slightly mad - but in hindsight, genius.

Enter Natasha Kaplinsky. A serious BBC newsreader with glossy hair and sharp diction, Natasha was an inspired choice. She brought credibility, class, and - as it turned out - a surprising amount of hip action. Paired with Brendan Cole, the smouldering Kiwi pro with a penchant for ignoring choreography notes, Natasha became the face of Series One. I remember watching them dance their first rumba and thinking, "This might actually work."

Then there was Lesley Garrett - opera singer, national treasure, and completely unafraid of a dramatic arm flourish. Her

11

musicality was a real asset, though her paso doble occasionally resembled a soprano chasing pigeons. She was partnered with Anton du Beke, who, even back then, had the smooth patter of a 1950s crooner and the patience of a saint. Their partnership felt like a slightly eccentric aunt and her charming nephew on a seaside holiday, which is to say: delightful.

The lineup continued with Christopher Parker, the *EastEnders* heartthrob, who brought in the teenage vote despite looking terrified most of the time; Claire Sweeney, all Liverpudlian warmth and killer timing; David Dickinson, orange of face but surprisingly light on his feet; and Jason Wood, a camp comic who gave it everything and left audiences in stitches, if not awe.

But the real stroke of genius came with Martin Offiah. Known as "Chariots" from his rugby league days, Offiah was physical, driven, and not exactly known for his elegance. That contrast - a powerhouse sportsman attempting a waltz - was exactly the kind of fish-out-of-water moment that *Strictly* would come to thrive on. He wasn't the best dancer, but he was game. And that mattered.

Behind the camera, the pressure to get the casting right was intense. A quiet word from someone in the know later told me that two other celebrities dropped out in the final week before filming. One cited "creative differences" (code for: didn't fancy being judged by Craig Revel Horwood), and the other panicked about the costume fitting. That gap meant frantic last-minute replacements, schedule reshuffles, and - according to one assistant producer - "a lot of biscuit eating and crying in stairwells."

But perhaps the most important casting decision wasn't a

celebrity at all - it was the pros. Back then, none of them were household names. Brendan Cole and Anton du Beke were arguably the most seasoned, but to most viewers, these were just impossibly fit strangers in tight shirts. Still, the show needed dancers who could not only perform but choreograph routines that made their partners look good - and handle the emotional rollercoaster of teaching someone with no rhythm how to execute a heel lead. It's not as easy as it looks.

In the months before the show aired, rehearsals began in makeshift studios across London. The pros were handed music selections, given the bare bones of a schedule, and told to whip their partners into shape. Some celebs were eager students. Others... not so much. One anonymous pro later admitted they spent the first week "just trying to convince their celeb to make eye contact in the mirror."

There were challenges, too. The BBC hadn't yet refined the now-familiar format, so rehearsal time was tight, technical resources were limited, and costume fittings were often squeezed into 20-minute slots between run-throughs. A common sight in the Elstree corridors: a celebrity in sequinned trousers eating a tuna sandwich and looking vaguely like they were going to be sick.

And yet, something special was already forming. Even in those early days, bonds were being made. Partnerships were forming. Walls were coming down. That magical *Strictly* alchemy - the mix of nerves, effort, and absolute exposure - was already turning this odd little show into something bigger than anyone expected.

What stands out most about the casting of Series One isn't that it was perfect - it wasn't - but that it had heart. The contestants were game. The pros were committed. And the show, in all its slightly wobbly, under-rehearsed glory, had soul. That's what pulled viewers in. We didn't want perfection. We wanted people to *try*. And try they did - with trembling arms, sweaty brows, and genuine bravery.

And let's not forget the judges. They too were cast - carefully, deliberately. We'll dive into their stories later, but it's worth noting here that their chemistry was part of the alchemy. Len Goodman: avuncular, fair, and utterly loveable. Arlene Phillips: passionate, exacting, with that dance-world pedigree. Craig Revel Horwood: deliciously sharp and never one to mince words. And Bruno Tonioli: the human embodiment of an exclamation mark.

Together, they brought balance. Praise and poison, encouragement and evisceration. It was theatre, and it worked.

Looking back, it's easy to mythologise that first cast. They weren't all brilliant. But they were brave. They took a punt on a show no one had ever seen before. They danced in fear, in joy, in earnest. And in doing so, they created the blueprint for the dozens of celebs who would follow.

Because *Strictly* isn't just about who can dance - it's about who's willing to.

And as we'll see next, it wasn't just the cast who faced challenges. The early production of *Strictly* was far from smooth sailing. Technical hiccups, costume crises, and the constant threat of total collapse... join me next as we explore the behind-

the-scenes chaos that somehow turned into a television triumph.

Early Challenges & Big Wins

If you've ever tried quickstepping on a freshly polished floor in
Cuban heels, you'll know: *even the best-laid routines can wobble.*
And in the early days of *Strictly Come Dancing*, there was plenty
of wobble - not just in the footwork, but in the production itself.
What we now know as a polished, high-gloss Saturday night
spectacular began its life as a mildly chaotic experiment held
together with hairpins, hope, and a whole lot of Velcro.

Behind the shimmering curtain and between those iconic opening titles, the first few weeks of *Strictly* were, to put it politely, a
bit of a mess. A loveable, well-meaning mess - but a mess all the
same. The production team were juggling an untested format,
a rotating cast of nervous celebrities, demanding professional
dancers, and the ever-present pressure of live TV. It's no
exaggeration to say that the fact the first series aired without a
major disaster was something of a miracle.

One of the earliest problems was the studio. Elstree Studios -
that legendary home of *EastEnders*, *Who Wants to Be a Million-
aire?*, and countless classic dramas - had the history, but not
necessarily the space. The set was cobbled together quickly,
and in those first rehearsals, dancers complained of slippery
floors, exposed cables, and sightlines that made spotting turns
all but impossible. At least two pros reportedly sprained ankles
before the live shows even began. In those early episodes, if you
rewatch carefully (and I have), you'll notice some dances seem

oddly confined. That's because they were. There simply wasn't room to go full foxtrot.

Then there was the issue of timing. Not musical timing - although that, too, was a work in progress - but the sheer logistics of staging the show live each week. Choreography had to be approved, costumes fitted, music arranged, lighting cues rehearsed, camera shots blocked, and all of it signed off before Saturday. Oh, and the celebs still had to learn their dances. It was a mad dash from Monday to showtime, with barely a moment to breathe. One producer described the mood as "controlled hysteria... but with glitter."

Technical glitches were common. On more than one occasion, the wrong track played in rehearsal. The lighting desk froze mid-run-through. One week, the autocue crashed entirely, leaving Bruce to ad-lib while backstage panicked and a stage-hand tried to reset the server with what I'm told was the same technique used to fix a dodgy toaster: unplug it and hope for the best. (Bruce, naturally, handled it like the consummate professional he was - you'd never have known.)

Costumes, too, were a source of drama. Without the now-enormous wardrobe team and glitter-stitching machinery that powers the show today, outfits were often handmade under pressure, with last-minute changes the norm. There's a rumour - and I have it on good authority - that one early celebrity had their trousers re-hemmed with double-sided tape minutes before going on air, only for the tape to fail during a jive. The resulting reveal was... memorable.

But for all the teething problems, something magical was happening.

The audiences - small, at first - responded. People weren't laughing *at* the show, they were rooting for it. Viewers connected with the vulnerability of the celebrities, the chemistry between the couples, and the genuine thrill of live performance. The unpredictability became part of the charm. When someone fluffed a step or forgot a count, it didn't break the illusion - it made it human.

And then came the first true *Strictly* moment. It wasn't perfect, technically speaking. It wasn't even a ten. But it was honest, moving, and powerful. Natasha Kaplinsky and Brendan Cole's week four waltz. Set to "Moon River," it was simple, elegant, and full of heart. When it ended, there was a beat - a pause in the studio - and then an eruption of applause that didn't feel polite or forced. It felt *earned.* I remember watching at home, holding my breath. That was the moment *Strictly* stopped being a novelty and started becoming a national treasure.

That week, the viewing figures jumped. The following Monday, tabloids printed stills from the dance. The *Radio Times* called it "surprisingly emotional." Ballroom, it seemed, was back.

But perhaps the biggest sign of success came in the most unexpected form: *the press stopped sneering.* In the lead-up to the show's debut, critics had written it off as a fluff piece, a weird blend of old-fashioned dancing and Z-list spectacle. But once it aired - and especially after those early high points - reviews became curious, then complimentary. Columnists who had mocked the concept found themselves debating foot placement. One famously sardonic critic even admitted: "I'm not sure what a rumba is, but I haven't missed an episode since."

And then there was the watercooler test. At work, at school, in supermarkets - people were *talking* about *Strictly*. Who looked nervous. Who nailed their routine. Who Craig was too harsh on. Suddenly, everyone had an opinion on hip action. That cultural shift - subtle at first, then explosive - was the beginning of what we now recognise as the *Strictly Effect*.

It wasn't just the public who took notice. Within the BBC, eyes widened. A Sunday night results show was introduced. Budget increased. The costume team was expanded. The production values rose dramatically by Series Two. And suddenly, *Strictly* wasn't a one-off experiment - it was a flagship.

But for me, the biggest early win was something less measurable: *emotion*. The show was funny, yes. Glamorous, absolutely. But more than anything, it was sincere. The celebrities were vulnerable. The pros were invested. The judges, for all their showmanship, *cared*. And that sincerity shone through the screen. You couldn't fake it. You didn't want to.

By the time Series One ended, with Natasha and Brendan hoisting the glitterball trophy under a shower of gold confetti, *Strictly Come Dancing* had done more than prove itself. It had *changed* something. It had brought ballroom back into living rooms. It had reminded us that live television could still surprise, still connect, still make us feel.

Looking back now, it's remarkable how close it all came to unravelling. A missed cue here, a misstep there, and the whole thing could've crumbled. But like any good routine, it held together - not because it was flawless, but because it had *heart*.

And with that, *Strictly* was off and running. From here, it would grow - in scale, in spectacle, in influence. But at its core, those early days remain a testament to what can happen when courage meets choreography.

And now that we've looked at where it began, it's time to meet the brave souls who step into the studio week after week, risking dignity and hamstrings in equal measure. The celebrities, yes - but more importantly, the ones who *make them stars*.

Next stop: the pros. The choreographers, the coaches, the calm amid the costume crisis. Let's lift the lid on the hardest-working high-kickers in showbiz.

4

Stars in Their Eyes (and Dancing Shoes)

What Makes a Great Strictly Contestant?

Every year, before the new series even begins, there's a kind of sacred ritual that unfolds in living rooms up and down the country. The lineup is announced - usually with much fanfare and a dramatic swirl of sparkles - and viewers immediately do what we've all been conditioned to do: judge. Not just who's on it, but how they'll do. "She'll be good, she was in that musical." "He's tall - bet he's got two left feet." "Never heard of her, she's going out first." And so the pre-show predictions begin.

But what *really* makes a great *Strictly* contestant? Is it rhythm? Personality? A sob story and a strong samba? Or is it something more elusive - a kind of sparkle that can't be taught?

Having watched every series (some more times than I'll publicly admit), and having taught dozens of dancers from trembling beginners to secret naturals, I've come to believe that the perfect *Strictly* contestant is not the one who arrives as a star. It's the one who *becomes* one.

You see, *Strictly* isn't just a dance competition. It's a transformation factory. It rewards growth, graft, and the kind of grit that doesn't always show up in the paso doble but does come through in the eyes of someone determined not to fall flat in front of fifteen million people. And the audience, bless us, *feels* that. We respond not to perfection, but to progress.

Some contestants show promise from day one. Think of Alesha Dixon, flying through her first cha-cha with natural rhythm and beaming charm. Or Louis Smith, whose athletic precision gave him instant presence. These are the ones people call "ringers" - those with performance backgrounds or dance-adjacent training. And yes, they often go far. But surprisingly, they don't always win hearts. Because what people really want is to *watch* someone change.

That's why a good contestant doesn't have to be the best dancer - but they *do* need a story. Not a scripted one, mind you, but a genuine journey. The shy person who comes out of their shell. The stiff one who finds fluidity. The joker who slowly reveals sincerity. These are the ones who capture the nation. We want to root for someone. And rooting means watching them stumble, improve, cry, laugh, and *try again*.

Bill Bailey is a perfect example. When he was announced, the general reaction was somewhere between confusion and amusement. A comedian? With eyebrows that move more than his feet? But week after week, he worked. He listened. He *danced*. And by the time he and Oti Mabuse lifted that glitterball in 2020, he'd become not just a great contestant – he'd become part of *Strictly* history.

And then, of course, there's likeability. A wildly subjective quality, but one that plays a huge part in a contestant's success. Because *Strictly* isn't judged solely by technical merit. The public has a vote – and the public is fickle. You can have the cleanest cha-cha in the business, but if viewers don't connect with you, you'll be waltzing home before Movie Week.

Conversely, some contestants hang on far longer than the leaderboard suggests they should, purely because they're loved. Ann Widdecombe. Ed Balls. Judy Murray. None were strong dancers. But they brought something else: personality. Entertainment. A willingness to laugh at themselves and still show up each week. That bravery – that self-aware, sequinned courage – is oddly captivating.

But charm alone isn't enough. To be truly great, a contestant needs to *respect* the process. The best ones take it seriously – not solemnly, but sincerely. They listen to their pros. They rehearse through tears and tantrums. They don't treat it like a joke, even if they know they won't win. And that respect shines through in the performance.

Rose Ayling-Ellis is a shining example. Her presence on the show broke barriers, shifted perceptions, and delivered some of the most emotionally resonant performances we've ever seen. Her silent segment during the couple's choice routine wasn't just beautiful – it was historic. But beyond the headlines, what made Rose such a phenomenal contestant was her grace, her focus, and her genuine love of learning. That's the magic formula.

And let's not forget resilience. The *Strictly* schedule is brutal. Rehearsals are relentless. Feedback is public and often harsh. Injuries happen. Nerves fray. One week you're flying high; the next, you're in the bottom two with a samba that made Craig raise his eyebrows so high they nearly left the studio. A great contestant takes the hits and comes back stronger.

It's why some celebs who seem like dead certs falter. They buckle under pressure. They lose heart. Or they simply don't adapt. Dance is as much about mindset as muscle memory. And those who can't shift into the rhythm of the show - emotionally as well as physically - tend to fall away.

I've always said that *Strictly* reveals character. The dance floor is unforgiving. You can't fake timing. You can't charm your way through a samba roll. But what you *can* do is show up. Try. Learn. Be present. Be brave. And when that happens - when a contestant embraces the challenge, connects with the audience, and grows before our eyes - that's when we fall in love.

So, what makes a great *Strictly* contestant?

Not fame. Not finesse. Not even footwork.

It's heart. It's hunger. It's humility. And maybe - just maybe - a bit of hip action.

And now that we've twirled through what makes a memorable contestant, it's time to lift the curtain on the casting process itself - the secret recipe of celebs, stories, and styles that keeps *Strictly* feeling fresh every single year.

The Casting Process Secrets

The moment *Strictly Come Dancing* announces its latest celebrity lineup has become something of a national sport. Twitter explodes. Breakfast shows speculate. Office WhatsApps light up with messages like, "Who's that?" or "They're going to be amazing." But few know just how meticulous - and surprisingly strategic - the casting process really is.

Contrary to popular belief, the *Strictly* lineup doesn't just fall together like confetti at a finale. Behind the scenes, it's a carefully choreographed affair, designed to hit a series of targets: personality types, age range, dance potential, story arcs, and - most importantly - audience connection. The team responsible doesn't just need famous faces. They need a *cast*. A full glittering spectrum of people the nation can root for, relate to, laugh at, and occasionally argue about over a Sunday roast.

Each year, months before the first sequin is sewn, a group of producers, talent bookers, and BBC executives gather to build what can only be described as the *Strictly* mosaic. They review lists of potential names, discuss trends, look at who's hot, who's nostalgic, and who might be a surprise hit. It's not unlike casting a film - only with more glitter and a higher chance of knee injury.

They start by aiming for a balance. One or two older contestants, a few younger ones, someone from soapland, a pop star, a newsreader, a wildcard, and at least one sports personality. Each category brings its own fanbase and flavour. Sports stars often have discipline and physicality. Soap actors bring familiarity and warmth. Musicians tend to have rhythm and stage confidence. Wildcards – comedians, politicians, novelty names – offer unpredictability and humour. It's a delicate ecosystem. Tip the balance too far in one direction and you risk alienating a chunk of the audience.

And then there's the "narrative factor." Producers look not just at names, but at *stories*. Who's on a comeback journey? Who's stepping outside their comfort zone? Who's just come through something significant – a divorce, a career shift, a public scandal? Viewers love a story. And *Strictly* is built around stories as much as steps.

It's why you often see someone "controversial" in the lineup – a tabloid regular, a reality TV villain, or someone who's had a difficult public image. The thinking is simple: give them the chance to show another side. Sometimes it works beautifully (see: Abbey Clancy). Sometimes it doesn't. But it always creates conversation.

The casting team also has to manage availability and logistics. It's not just about who *wants* to do the show – it's about who *can*. *Strictly* is a huge time commitment: weeks of rehearsals, press appearances, costume fittings, and long, long Saturdays. Celebrities in the middle of touring or filming often can't make the schedule work, no matter how enthusiastic they are. And then there are insurance issues, existing contracts, and the all-important NDA paperwork. It's a dance of its own, and not always a graceful one.

Interestingly, the producers also keep a "longlist" of names each year – people who've been considered before or expressed interest in the past. Some celebs have been in talks for *years* before finally signing on. Others flirt with the idea, get close to the fitting room, and then back away when the reality (and the rhinestones) set in. I've heard tales of celebrities who agreed in principle, only to bolt at the first sight of Latin heels. One famously asked if they could do the show "without being judged," which rather misses the point.

And then there are those who turn it down flat. Some fear humiliation. Others worry about injuries. A few simply can't handle the exposure. But some - and I know this from first-hand whispers - regret their decision the moment the series airs and someone *else* becomes a breakout star. There's nothing quite like watching another celeb steal the nation's heart to make you second-guess your choice.

Once the casting team locks in their final list, the pairing process begins. It's not just about height and build (although that matters - no one wants a jive with a foot difference between partners). It's about chemistry, energy, and how their personalities complement each other. A shy contestant might be paired with an enthusiastic pro to bring them out of their shell. A fiery celeb might need a calm, experienced hand. And occasionally, a producer will roll the dice with a wildcard combo, just to see what sparks.

Some pros are heavily involved in the casting process - not in choosing their partner, but in feeding back on rehearsal styles, preferences, and coaching approaches. The team works hard to avoid clashes in teaching style or temperament. Of course, they don't always get it right. But when a pairing works, it *really* works. Just ask Stacey and Kevin.

Another layer to the casting process is diversity - something *Strictly* has worked hard to improve in recent years. That includes racial representation, age range, LGBTQ+ inclusion, and most notably, ability. When Rose Ayling-Ellis joined the show, it was a landmark moment. She wasn't just included – she was *centred*. Her presence expanded what the show could be. It wasn't tokenistic. It was transformative.

And that's the other secret of the casting process: evolution. The producers don't just cast for *this* year – they think about how each season moves the show forward. What new ground is broken? What story hasn't been told yet? How can *Strictly* remain familiar, but not stale?

Even the reveal process is part of the strategy. Celebs are often announced one by one over several days – on radio shows, chat shows, social media. This keeps the buzz building. Fans speculate, guess, debate. It becomes a national guessing game. And by the time the full list is out, the season already feels like it's begun.

Casting, in the end, is both art and alchemy. It's about more than big names. It's about the balance of personalities, stories, and potential. The best lineups aren't the ones with the most famous people. They're the ones that *click*. That feel like a Saturday night dinner party with guests you didn't expect to love – but do.

Next, we'll revisit some of those surprise stars. The ones who didn't just show up – they shone. The memorable contestants who became part of *Strictly* lore, whether they won the trophy or not.

And trust me, some of them will surprise you.

Memorable Celebs Through the Years

Over two decades of *Strictly Come Dancing* have given us plenty of glitter, gallons of fake tan, and more feathered paso costumes than the BBC wardrobe department ever dreamed possible. But beneath the sparkle, the show's real legacy lives in the contestants who've left their mark - not just with their scores, but with their *stories*. Some waltzed in with fanfare. Others arrived quietly and captured our hearts. A few tripped over their own feet and still walked away national treasures.

Let's take a moment to remember the ones we'll never forget - the unforgettable celebrities who've danced their way into *Strictly* history, not necessarily because they were the best, but because they were the most *memorable*.

When people talk about *Strictly* icons, they often start with **Mark Ramprakash**. On paper, the idea of a cricketer delivering Latin fire seemed unlikely. But from the moment he hit the floor with Karen Hardy, something clicked. Their chemistry was electric, their routines thrilling. And when their salsa was interrupted by a technical hiccup - the mic pack coming loose - they stopped, regrouped, and restarted without flinching. That moment, and the grace with which they handled it, sealed their legend. They went on to win the series, of course - but what people remember is the resilience and that crowd-roaring re-do.

Then there's **Jill Halfpenny**, whose jive with Darren Bennett remains, to this day, one of the most celebrated dances in *Strictly* history. It was sharp, energetic, and completely joyous - everything the show wanted to be. Jill wasn't a total novice, having come from a theatre background, but her journey was still compelling. She trained hard, improved each week, and won hearts as well as scores. The best part? She made it *look* like fun.

But it's not all about the winners. Some of the most memorable celebs are the ones who didn't come close to the glitterball - and didn't need to.

Take **Ann Widdecombe**, for example. Was she a good dancer? Absolutely not. Did she become a national talking point? Without question. Her routines with Anton du Beke were less about footwork and more about flying, flapping, and facial expressions. She was hoisted, dragged, spun, and in one memorable moment, descended from the ceiling in a harness like a sequin-drenched Christmas angel. Purists groaned. Viewers howled. And the ratings soared. Like it or not, Ann became a *Strictly* icon - proof that sometimes, personality *can* out-dance technique.

In a similar (but far more endearing) vein, **Ed Balls**. No one expected the former shadow chancellor to set the floor alight. But his journey - from political punchline to jive-performing, Gangnam-Styling national uncle - was one of the most charming arcs the show has ever delivered. Partnered with Katya Jones, Ed gave it everything: hips, heart, and humour. His Salsa to "Gangnam Style" will go down in TV history - not because it was good, but because it was unforgettable.

And let's not forget the truly transformative contestants - the ones who not only learned to dance, but discovered something about themselves along the way.

29

Stacey Dooley is a perfect example. Known for her hard-hitting documentaries, she entered the show with a certain scepticism – and left it a winner, in every sense. Her chemistry with Kevin Clifton was real, her growth was visible, and her performances, particularly her Paso Doble and show dance, were full of strength and elegance. More than that, though, she showed the audience a different side of herself – softer, lighter, still driven, but dancing from joy.

Rose Ayling-Ellis, of course, redefined what the show could be. As the first deaf contestant, her participation was historic – but it was her talent, determination, and sheer grace that made her unforgettable. Partnered with Giovanni Pernice, Rose didn't just dance – she *moved* people. Their Couple's Choice routine, which featured a silent segment to honour the deaf community, wasn't just powerful television – it was art. It won them the glitterball and a permanent place in the show's history.

Bill Bailey proved that age and occupation needn't define you. As a middle-aged comic with a penchant for prog rock, he seemed an unlikely frontrunner. But with Oti Mabuse's brilliant choreography and his own dedication, Bill became a beacon of surprise brilliance. His Couple's Choice to Rapper's Delight? Joyous. His Tango? Fierce. His win? Deserved. He shattered expectations and became a symbol of late-in-life learning and celebration.

Then there are the heartbreakers – the ones who *should* have won, or at least stayed longer, but left us too soon.

Danny Mac, who danced with Oti Mabuse in 2016, was a technical marvel. His Samba alone earned the highest praise from the judges, and rightly so. He was fluid, powerful, and controlled. But sometimes, great dancing isn't enough – the final vote just didn't swing his way.

Ashley Roberts was another technically stunning contestant, often criticised for being "too good" because of her Pussycat Dolls background. But the way she grew emotionally – the raw nerves behind the polished routines – made her story just as valid. She didn't win, but she left a powerful impression.

And then there are those who blossomed late.

Hamza Yassin, for example, wasn't on many people's winner lists at the beginning. But week after week, his gentle charm, unexpected grace, and breathtaking lifts with Jowita Przystał turned him into a fan favourite – and eventual champion. His win reminded us all that *Strictly* is never just about first impressions.

Some contestants win the trophy. Others win hearts. And the most memorable do both – not by being perfect, but by being present. Honest. Brave. Willing to learn and laugh and occasionally fall over in front of millions.

Because that's the real magic of *Strictly*. It's not about who you were before the show. It's about who you become during it.

And for every celebrity who has slipped on those dance shoes and stepped onto that iconic floor, there's been one constant: the pros who guide them, push them, carry them – sometimes literally – across the finish line. They are the backbone of the show, the unsung heroes in heels and hard graft.

Next, we go backstage into the rehearsal rooms, the late-night run-throughs, the sore feet, and the big personalities. It's time to meet the professionals.

And trust me, darling - they're more than just legs.

5

The Professionals – More Than Just Legs

Life Before the Glitterball

They spin. They lift. They glide across the floor like it's made of clouds and good decisions. But long before they were Sunday-night superstars, before the costumes and cameras, the professionals of *Strictly Come Dancing* were just dancers. Dancers with aching feet, relentless ambition, and a dream so persistent it outlasted the bruises. To understand the magic they bring to the ballroom now, we need to understand where they came from - and what they sacrificed to get here.

Professional dancers are often born in the studio. Not literally, although I wouldn't be surprised - but many start young. As in *five-years-old, miniature leotard, too-small tap shoes* young. The early years are filled with plies, pirouettes, posture drills, and an alarming number of hours spent being told to "try it again, but better." While most kids are mastering handwriting, these future pros are learning heel leads and head placement. It's discipline, it's devotion - and it's not for the faint of heart.

By the time they're teenagers, they're already veterans of the dance floor. While their classmates are at house parties and awkward school discos, they're in competitions - often travelling across countries in a blur of glitter hairspray and garment bags. Ballroom and Latin dancers in particular are part of a fierce, insular circuit. Championships are intense. Politics run deep. The stakes feel enormous. And yet, for many of these dancers, it's the only world they've ever known - and the only one they want.

Anton du Beke, for instance, started training in his teens and quickly found a love for the classic structure of ballroom. He once said in an interview that dancing gave him a sense of belonging - a place where the rules were clear and the expectations high. That sentiment is echoed by many of his fellow pros. Dance isn't just a job. It's an identity.

Before *Strictly*, many of the show's professionals had already built formidable careers. Brendan Cole competed internationally and trained with the best of the best. Karen Hardy was a world champion in Latin American dance. Camilla Dallerup was a top contender on the competitive scene long before she joined the show. These were dancers at the *top* of their game, often with accolades and reputations to match - just not in the public eye. They were stars in a closed world, waiting for their moment to break into the open.

And then came that moment. In 2004, when the first series of

Strictly Come Dancing was announced, a casting call went out to the ballroom elite. The producers weren't just looking for great dancers. They were looking for choreographers, teachers, performers – people who could entertain as well as educate. It wasn't enough to execute a perfect cha-cha. You had to be able to *teach* it to a nervous soap star in six days, then perform it live in front of millions with a smile on your face and a glitter explosion at your feet.

It was, quite frankly, a terrifying proposition.

Some dancers jumped at the chance. Others hesitated. The competitive ballroom world is fiercely traditional. To many, *Strictly* seemed... well, undignified. Reality television? Celebrities? Public voting? It all sounded terribly unserious. But a handful of visionaries saw the opportunity – not just for their own careers, but for ballroom itself. This was a chance to take their beloved, often niche art form and beam it into millions of homes. To make it *matter* again.

The early professionals had no guarantees. They didn't know if the show would last. They didn't know if the public would embrace ballroom or mock it. They were taking a risk. But they showed up – sequins, nerves and all – and in doing so, changed the course of their careers forever.

And of course, not all pros came from the competitive circuit. Some had more commercial or theatrical backgrounds. Take Flavia Cacace, whose elegance and storytelling made her a fan favourite. Or Oti Mabuse, who trained across multiple disciplines, bringing a contemporary edge to her choreography. The show began to draw in dancers from all corners of the world – Cuba, South Africa, Russia, Italy – each bringing their own flavour, style, and cultural stamp to the British ballroom.

What's remarkable is how many of these dancers didn't just *survive* the transition to TV - they *thrived* in it. Being a pro on *Strictly* requires a specific blend of attributes: technical excellence, teaching ability, on-camera charm, emotional intelligence, physical endurance, and - crucially - patience. Imagine trying to teach a samba to someone who has never danced before and is terrified of rhythm. Then do it again, next week. With a new routine. For three months.

The job is relentless. But before they were *Strictly* pros, these dancers had already learned relentless.

And yet, many of them will tell you that *Strictly* is the most rewarding chapter of their careers. Not just because of the fame - though that certainly helps pay for the physio - but because of what it represents. For the first time, the work they've done for decades is *seen*. Valued. Celebrated. They're not just background dancers. They're choreographers. Partners. Coaches. Sometimes therapists. And always artists.

And let's be clear - it's not just about teaching the celebs. These dancers are *performers* in their own right. The professional group numbers are often some of the most breathtaking moments of the series - technically brilliant, emotionally charged, and visually spectacular. When they take the stage without their celeb partners, you see the full power of their talent. It's a reminder that before they were teaching sambas to sports presenters, they were stars in their own spotlight.

In recent years, we've seen many pros become household names in their own right. Anton, of course, is now a judge. Oti Mabuse became a brand unto herself, with appearances across the BBC and ITV. Johannes Radebe has become a symbol of joy, resilience, and representation. These dancers have transcended their original roles and become something bigger – ambassadors for dance, for expression, and for the beauty of movement.

But what connects them all – from Series One veterans to the latest arrivals – is where they came from. The hours in cold studios. The blisters and back injuries. The missed birthdays, the rehearsed routines, the endless music cues. Long before the glitterball, there was graft. There still is.

And that's why we love them.

Next, we'll step into the rehearsal rooms and the emotionally charged world of celeb-pro partnerships – where patience is tested, breakthroughs are made, and sometimes... the magic really begins.

Ready to meet them behind the scenes?

Coaching Celebs, Dodging Drama

If the ballroom is the show, then the rehearsal studio is the war room. It's where battles are fought, victories are earned, tears are shed, and occasionally, Latin hips are discovered against all odds. Every Saturday night performance begins here – in a dance studio with mirrored walls, battered floors, and enough emotional energy to power a West End run. Because while the audience sees the glitz, the grace, and the standing ovations, what they *don't* see is the graft. And trust me, there's a *lot* of it.

Coaching a celebrity on *Strictly* is not like coaching a trained dancer. It's not even like teaching a beginner in your average ballroom class. This is an entirely different beast - a crash course in discipline, diplomacy, and deep breathing. The pro has one week to turn a terrified celebrity into a competent performer, capable of executing choreography under pressure, in costume, in front of millions. And then they have to do it again the next week. With a different dance. From scratch.

The first rehearsal is often the most telling. The celeb walks into the studio with nervous energy, armed with water bottles, knee supports, and - more often than not - a well-rehearsed speech about having "two left feet." The pro, clipboard in hand, smiles reassuringly and starts the assessment. Rhythm? Posture? Coordination? Can they hear the beat? Can they move their feet without tripping over their own self-esteem?

Some celebs surprise you. They pick things up quickly, ask good questions, and respond to coaching. Others... need work. I've heard stories from pros who've spent the entire first session just trying to get their partner to *walk* to music. Not dance - just *walk*. To the beat. In a straight line. It sounds simple. It isn't.

Then comes the choreography. Each week, the pros have to design a routine that ticks a dizzying list of boxes:

- It must follow the rules of the dance style.
- It must highlight the celeb's strengths (and cleverly disguise their weaknesses).
- It must be entertaining and fit the music.
- It must impress the judges and win over the voting public.
- And it must be teachable - in about four and a half days.

That's right – contrary to what you might imagine, most couples only get **four or five days** of proper rehearsal time. Sundays are often filled with interviews, costume fittings, and rest. Mondays to Thursdays are the real workdays, and Friday is the camera run-through at Elstree. So the clock is *always* ticking.

Some celebs respond well to this pressure. They come in early, stay late, drill routines until they're dizzy. Others... struggle. Rehearsals can be emotionally charged. Tempers flare. Doubts creep in. Tears happen – on both sides. One pro once told me they cried in a toilet cubicle after a Thursday session where their partner "forgot every single step for the third time that morning." It's not uncommon.

What makes it work – what keeps the process moving – is the *relationship* between the celeb and the pro. Chemistry isn't just for the dance floor. In the rehearsal studio, it's the difference between connection and combustion. Some partnerships click instantly. There's mutual respect, banter, shared humour. Others take longer. Occasionally, the energy is tense – polite, but distant. And in rare cases, it's downright difficult.

The producers do their best to pair celebs and pros based on complementary personalities, but it's still a gamble. You're essentially locking two people in a room together for twelve hours a day and asking them to perform miracles. It's no wonder some of them snap.

But the good ones – the great partnerships – are where the real Strictly gold lives.

Think of **Rose and Giovanni**. The trust between them was palpable from day one. He learned sign language to communicate better. She trusted him completely. The result? Poetry in motion - and a victory that felt earned in every sense.

Or **Kelvin Fletcher and Oti Mabuse**, a last-minute replacement pairing that became a powerhouse. Their samba in week one remains one of the most explosive series openers in *Strictly* history. But behind that was a week of intense, nonstop rehearsals. Oti pushed. Kelvin delivered. The chemistry? Electric.

Then there are the "opposites attract" duos - like **Ed Balls and Katya Jones**. She, a fierce technician with a bold choreographic eye. He, a lovable dad with the rhythm of a startled penguin. But somehow, they made it work. Katya leaned into comedy. Ed leaned into Katya. The result? TV gold.

What all these partnerships have in common is *balance*. The pro becomes a coach, a motivator, a friend, and occasionally, a therapist. They learn how to read their celeb's mood. When to push. When to pause. When to abandon a tricky spin and go back to basics. It's not just about dancing - it's about *trust*.

Trust, of course, isn't always easy. Especially when things go wrong. Missed cues. Memory blanks. Physical exhaustion. Injuries. Not every week is a triumph. Some routines bomb. Some feedback stings. Some rehearsals end in silence. But when a celeb picks themselves back up - and when the pro guides them through that moment - something shifts. That's when the audience starts to *feel* the journey.

One of the great unsung skills of a *Strictly* pro is their ability to protect their celeb - emotionally, physically, and reputationally. They hold space. They shield. They encourage. And they keep the show on track, even when everything feels wobbly. That emotional labour is invisible on-screen, but it's a huge part of the job.

And sometimes, it goes beyond the studio. Friendships form. Partnerships endure. Kevin and Stacey. Gorka and Gemma. Kristina and Joe. Even when romance isn't involved, the bond between celeb and pro often lasts long after the glitter settles. They've been through something intense together - something public, vulnerable, and strangely profound.

But it's not all emotional catharsis and soulful chats over protein bars. There are *plenty* of hilarious moments too. Wardrobe malfunctions. Accidental lifts. Rehearsal room giggles that derail entire sessions. One pro told me their celeb once got so dizzy during a spin that they fell into a clothes rail and emerged with a feather boa wrapped around their neck - which they then refused to take off for the rest of rehearsal because it made them "feel more graceful."

Coaching on *Strictly* is a delicate dance of its own - one that requires patience, empathy, adaptability, and a wicked sense of humour. It's about seeing potential where others see panic. It's about finding the rhythm in someone who swears they have none. And most of all, it's about celebrating progress, not perfection.

Next, we'll look beyond the rehearsal rooms and into the spotlight - to the pro dancers themselves. Their identities, their personal styles, and how they became *Strictly* legends in their own right.

Icons of the Ballroom

They may have started as background dancers, supporting the glitter-flecked journeys of nervy celebs. But over twenty dazzling seasons, the professional dancers on *Strictly Come Dancing* have become icons in their own right - household names, national treasures, and in some cases, walking sequins. They've inspired, entertained, and reinvented what it means to be a dancer on primetime TV. This is their moment in the spotlight.

Let's start with the originals - the founding figures of *Strictly's* professional pantheon. When the show launched in 2004, it brought with it a handful of dancers who would become *Strictly* royalty. **Anton du Beke**, for example, wasn't just a dancer - he was a charming, old-school showman with impeccable timing and more tails than a West End costume cupboard. From the moment he glided across the floor in Series One, Anton became the face of traditional ballroom, beloved by viewers for his wit, warmth, and unwavering elegance.

Alongside him were dancers like **Erin Boag**, with her razor-sharp foxtrots and classic glamour; **Camilla Dallerup**, whose chemistry with celeb partners was undeniable; and **Brendan Cole**, the original *Strictly* bad boy - all smoulder and sass, with a cha-cha that could cut glass. These early pros helped establish the tone of the show: technical brilliance paired with full-on personality.

As the show grew, so did the cast. Each new generation of professionals brought a fresh flavour - new styles, diverse backgrounds, and different interpretations of what it meant to be a "Strictly pro." Some came from the ballroom world. Others from commercial dance, Latin theatre, or international stages. All of them had to find their groove - not just on the floor, but in the hearts of the audience.

Janette Manrara, for example, won fans with her boundless energy and passionate performances. She wasn't just a brilliant dancer - she was pure *joy* in motion. **Aljaž Škorjanec**, her real-life husband, became equally adored for his charisma, cheeky charm, and enviable hips. They brought love to the floor - literally - and reminded us that *Strictly* is, at its core, about connection.

Then there's **Oti Mabuse**. With her sharp choreography, fearless performances, and glowing presence, Oti redefined what it meant to be a pro. She wasn't just teaching - she was storytelling. Her routines with Kelvin Fletcher and Bill Bailey weren't just technically dazzling - they were *narrative events*, full of character, humour, and unexpected depth. Her back-to-back wins cemented her as one of the greats - and opened the door for her to become a household name beyond *Strictly*.

Some pros made waves with their style. **Giovanni Pernice** brought a mix of Latin heat and emotional vulnerability, creating some of the show's most iconic moments (Rose Ayling-Ellis, anyone?). **Johannes Radebe** made headlines and history - not just with his moves, but with his unapologetic joy, his ground-breaking same-sex partnership with John Whaite, and his ability to turn every paso doble into a manifesto for self-expression.

Others have become quietly legendary - beloved not for flash, but for their consistency, warmth, and understated magic.

Karen Hauer, with her fierce technique and rock-solid coaching style, has partnered everyone from Mark Wright to Jamie Laing. **Dianne Buswell**, with her technicolour hair and genuine connection to fans, brings heart and humour to every routine. These are dancers who have built legacies over seasons - not just through wins, but through presence.

And let's not forget the group numbers - a place where pros truly *let loose*. These show-stopping medleys are where we see the full power of their artistry. Freed from teaching duties, the dancers become headliners, pushing boundaries with bold themes, edgy choreography, and breathtaking visuals. Whether it's a James Bond tango or a Bridgerton-inspired Viennese waltz, the pros take these numbers to new heights - creating mini-musicals that wouldn't look out of place on Broadway.

But beyond the steps and the sparkle, what makes these professionals *iconic* is their emotional presence. They're not just athletes - they're *storytellers*. Every lift, every glance, every final pose is part of a narrative. They dance joy, sorrow, triumph, and heartbreak - often on behalf of their partners. They make us *feel*.

They've also become role models - for kids who want to dance, for young pros dreaming of TV stardom, and for viewers who've never waltzed a step but believe, just for a moment, that they *could*. Their presence on *Strictly* has expanded the definition of who belongs on the dancefloor. Black dancers, queer dancers, dancers with diverse body types - all have taken their place in the spotlight, and in doing so, made the ballroom a more inclusive, exciting space.

Some pros move on. They choreograph, judge, or star in other shows. Anton is now a judge. Oti fronts primetime telly. Janette co-hosts *It Takes Two*. But their roots are always in *Strictly*. And fans never forget. The legacy of a *Strictly* pro doesn't end with their final waltz. It lives on in the routines we rewatch, the journeys we remember, and the joy they bring to the nation, one heel-turn at a time.

In a show full of celebrities, it's the professionals who keep the heartbeat steady. They teach. They train. They shine. And they carry the very soul of *Strictly Come Dancing* in every eight-count.

Next, we pivot away from the professionals and into the glitzy, glittery world of *costume*. Because darling, the dance is only half the drama – the other half is stitched in sequins and delivered on a coat hanger.

6

Sequins, Spray Tans & Wardrobe Whirlwinds

Dressing for Drama – The Art of the Strictly Look

I f *Strictly Come Dancing* is a fairytale, then the wardrobe department are the fairy godmothers – stitching dreams from satin, sequins, and Swarovski stones. Because before a single heel hits the dancefloor, a transformation must take place. One moment you're a soap star in a tracksuit – the next, you're a samba queen in feathers, rhinestones, and lashes that could sweep the studio.

Costume is not a side note on *Strictly* – it's part of the performance. It shapes mood, signals style, and elevates the entire experience from televised talent show to full-blown Saturday night spectacle. And like everything else on the show, it's delivered on an eye-wateringly tight schedule.

Let's start with the process. Each week, the wardrobe team – headed by the ever-brilliant **Vicky Gill** and her crack squad of designers, stylists, and seamstresses – are tasked with creating upwards of 20 bespoke costumes. From concept to camera, they have less than seven days. It's a creative sprint, not a leisurely saunter.

Monday mornings begin with choreography meetings. The pros meet with producers, music supervisors, and the costume team to pitch the concept for that week's dance. Is it a romantic rumba set in 1940s Paris? A paso doble with matador vibes? A samba straight from Rio Carnival? Whatever the vibe, wardrobe must translate that into *fabric*.

Sketches are drawn. Fabrics sourced. Colours chosen. Sparkle levels discussed. And then the magic begins. Unlike most fashion design, these costumes aren't just about looking good – they must *move*, *survive lifts*, and accommodate everything from cartwheels to quicksteps. They're essentially athletic gear masquerading as haute couture.

Once the concept is approved, fittings begin. And this is where the fun – and sometimes chaos – begins.

Imagine wrangling a celeb who's never worn sequins before, has two left feet, and is mildly allergic to lycra – and you have three days to make them feel like a dancefloor demigod. That's the weekly miracle the wardrobe team pulls off.

Some celebrities embrace the process. They dive into the feathers, embrace the sparkle, and say yes to the fake tan with glee. Others... need encouragement. I've heard stories of celebs nearly walking out over a revealing top, or panicking over being "put in pink." One male celeb reportedly told Vicky Gill, "I don't *do* glitter." Vicky, ever the professional, smiled sweetly and said, "Darling, glitter *does* you."

But time and again, the costume wins them over. Because when it works - when the fabric flatters, the colour pops, and the mirror reflects someone *new* - something shifts. Posture changes. Confidence grows. And suddenly, that terrified celeb is ready to tango.

There's a psychological element too. Costumes help *tell the story* of the dance. A dramatic paso needs drama in the skirt. A Charleston needs fringe to flap. A Viennese waltz calls for romance, flowing sleeves, and soft pastels. Costume isn't just decoration - it's narrative.

Take **Rose Ayling-Ellis and Giovanni's Couple's Choice** - the one where the music dropped out and they danced in silence. Her costume was simple, soft, elegant. Nothing distracted from the emotional message. Or **Caroline Flack's Argentine tango**, where a sleek, dark costume elevated the rawness of the routine. These weren't just outfits - they were *characters*.

And the wardrobe team doesn't just dress the couples. They design for the pro numbers, the judges, the presenters, and even the backing dancers. Claudia Winkleman's monochrome chic? Tess Daly's floor-length glamour? All part of the machine - one that churns out looks worthy of the red carpet, week after week.

Let's not forget the legendary *theme weeks*. Movie Week? That's 20 characters to design from scratch. Halloween Week? Add cobwebs, fangs, and fake blood to the equation. Musicals Week? You need Broadway panache with ballroom practicality. It's a logistical high-wire act - and yet, year after year, the team delivers.

Of course, things don't always go to plan. Hemlines fall. Zips break. One dancer famously lost a shoe mid-salsa and finished barefoot without missing a beat. Another ripped a seam mid-jive and had to hold their trousers up with one hand for the final eight counts. But the show goes on - and the wardrobe team is always backstage with safety pins, sewing machines, and nerves of steel.

Then there's the fake tan. Ah, the *Strictly* tan - as essential as the cha-cha. Every celeb gets bronzed within an inch of their life, regardless of skin tone, season, or personal protest. It's part of the glow. The tan makes muscles pop, defines movement, and adds that healthy, "just got back from rehearsals in Marbella" vibe that the audience now expects.

Fake tan is applied religiously - sometimes daily. And let me tell you, it gets *everywhere*. Dressing rooms, doorknobs, the inside of white shirts - nothing is safe. But it's all part of the Strictly ritual. Tan on. Glitter up. Hair high. Lashes long. And suddenly, you're not yourself anymore. You're a performer.

That transformation - from civilian to showstopper - is one of the secret joys of *Strictly*. And costume is the catalyst. It's not vanity. It's *alchemy*. Fabric becomes confidence. Fringe becomes freedom. And sequins? Well, sequins are stardust, darling.

In the next section, we head behind the velvet curtain and meet the army of unsung heroes who make all this sparkle happen - the makeup artists, hair stylists, floor managers, and coffee runners who turn chaos into choreography.

Let's meet the machine that makes the magic.

Shall we step backstage?

Backstage Pass – Meet the Crew Who Make It Happen

It's 6:05 PM on a Saturday. In ten minutes, millions of viewers will be watching. Celebrities are still rehearsing their footwork. A feather boa is shedding like a moulting flamingo. Someone's lost a shoe. And backstage? Controlled mayhem. It takes a village to raise a performance – and *Strictly Come Dancing* has one of the most hardworking, unsung villages in British television.

We tend to focus on the judges, the dancers, the glitterball trophy – but truthfully, none of it would work without the backstage crew. They're the invisible heartbeat of *Strictly*, running the show with split-second precision, steady nerves, and an astonishing ability to apply false eyelashes while holding a clipboard.

Let's start with the **hair and makeup team**, whose salon setups backstage resemble something between a backstage fashion show and a magician's dressing room. Led by the indomitable **Lisa Armstrong** and her team of spray-wielding stylists, this crew transforms everyday humans into showbiz royalty. They don't just "do hair" – they sculpt, spray, backcomb, and occasionally glitter-bomb until everyone looks camera-ready.

Makeup is done in shifts – often with the clock ticking and nerves jangling. The team must match looks to dance styles, costumes, and lighting, all while managing fidgety celebrities who may or may not have had three hours' sleep. Smoky eyes for a tango, bold lip for a samba, dewy glow for a waltz - and it all has to stay put under hot lights and heavy movement.

Hair is a masterpiece of engineering. Think buns that defy gravity, ponytails that can withstand pirouettes, and curls that survive the cha-cha. The team often has less than twenty minutes to take someone from "rehearsal scruffy" to "red carpet ready" - and they do it while laughing, listening, and hyping the nervous wreck in the chair.

Next, we glide over to the **floor managers and studio crew**. If hair and makeup are the sparkle, these are the gears. Every dance is a logistical ballet: set pieces must be placed, removed, and rearranged between performances. One minute it's a Viennese gazebo, the next it's a neon disco floor. These shifts happen in seconds - in total silence, in low light, and often under extreme pressure.

The floor managers communicate by headsets, hand signals, and - if all else fails - a good old-fashioned stage whisper. They guide dancers to their marks, ensure the judges' desk doesn't topple mid-lift, and make sure that no celebrity accidentally exits stage left and wanders into *EastEnders.* They are the calm in the sequinned storm.

Now, let's hear it for the **lighting and effects team**, unsung artists who turn each dance into a cinematic spectacle. These are the wizards behind the dramatic spotlights, twinkling fairy-tale hues, and those sweeping camera cranes that make every paso look like a movie finale. They collaborate with choreographers to match each routine's energy, shifting colour palettes to signal mood - moody blue for a slow waltz, fiery red for a salsa, golden glow for a foxtrot finale.

And who's calling all these shots? Enter the **gallery crew** - the producers, directors, vision mixers, and script supervisors hidden away in a tech-laden booth. They're the ones choosing which camera angle to cut to mid-dance, when to zoom in on a teary celeb, and when to cue the glitter cannon. They sit with headsets glued to ears, juggling multiple feeds, timing graphics, and whispering sweet nothings like "Camera 4 on Shirley, now!" into the void.

Behind every judge's comment is a script team, keeping the show on track. Behind every presenter's link is an autocue operator. Behind every celebrity crying into Claudia's shoulder is someone with tissues just off-camera.

And then there's **wardrobe quick-change assistants**, affectionately known backstage as the *sequin paramedics*. If a dance is going to costume change mid-show - say, removing a skirt layer, replacing a shirt, or switching accessories - these folks do it with Formula 1 pit-stop speed. I've seen them rip off trousers, replace jackets, and apply body glitter all in under 30 seconds.

Props crew, too, deserve medals. Those candy canes in Musicals Week? That full-scale pirate ship in Movie Week? Someone built it. Someone rolled it out. Someone stored it behind the fog machine when it wasn't on screen.

Even the **catering and hospitality crew** deserve their flowers. Rehearsals are gruelling. Energy drops. Tempers flare. And suddenly, a tray of sandwiches or a cup of builder's tea can save a partnership - or at least prevent a diva moment. These teams know the cast's favourite snacks, caffeine requirements, and how to deliver them with minimum fuss and maximum cheer.

Let's not forget the **runners** - the Swiss Army knives of the backstage world. They do everything from fetching forgotten trainers to escorting celebs from rehearsals to the studio. They carry clipboards, emergency tights, and the emotional weight of five dance-off nerves at once.

And what ties all of this together? Teamwork. Backstage on *Strictly* is a choreography of its own - a thousand small movements working in harmony to deliver two hours of seamless entertainment. Every crew member knows their role. Every mistake is covered within seconds. Every performance is supported by dozens of invisible hands.

The real magic of *Strictly* isn't just what happens under the glitterball - it's what happens in the shadows around it. The quiet professionalism. The whispered encouragements. The duct tape. So much duct tape.

And while we're busy clapping for the celebs and pros on Saturday night, somewhere backstage, someone's holding a shoe, mopping a forehead, or frantically sewing on a button that fell off five seconds before the music starts.

Next, we peel off the glitter and step into the rehearsal room - where the real work happens. It's not just spray tans and sequins. It's sweat, tears, arguments, breakthroughs - and the incredible transformations that turn average Joes into dancing legends.

Rehearsals, Rivalries & the Road to Saturday Night

If Saturday night is the performance, Monday to Friday is the proving ground. For every perfectly timed tango or sizzling samba you see under the glitterball, there are hours - *days* - of sweat, swearing, sore feet, and the occasional emotional meltdown behind it. Welcome to the *Strictly* rehearsal room, where stars are born, backs are strained, and relationships are pushed to the limit.

Each week, the clock resets. Regardless of last week's scores or standing ovations, it all starts again on Monday. New dance. New music. New routine. And usually, a new set of challenges. For the celebrity contestants, many of whom have never danced a step in their lives, this cycle is relentless - exhilarating, yes, but also utterly exhausting.

Let's begin with the **Monday meetings**. The pros and celebs are told what dance they've drawn for the week. Some cheer. Others groan. There's always one who mutters, "I was *really* hoping it wouldn't be the samba." Tough luck, love - it's in the dance card now.

From there, the pros go into overdrive. They choreograph bespoke routines tailored to their partner's strengths (and many, many weaknesses). Can't spin? Replace with a lift. Struggles with hip action? Build in some cheeky character work. The pros are masters at creative disguise - turning limitations into crowd-pleasing flair.

Rehearsals are held in dance studios across the country - London, Manchester, sometimes hotel conference rooms if they're on tour. The hours are brutal. Some couples train six, eight, even ten hours a day. And it's not just the steps they're learning. It's posture. Frame. Timing. Technique. Muscle memory.

The early days of training are often physical comedy gold. I remember watching a very famous newsreader trying to master a Viennese waltz turn and instead spinning into the mirror, arms flailing like a wind turbine in a hurricane. That same newsreader later got two tens for his foxtrot - proof that miracles *do* happen in the *Strictly* studio.

But it's not all giggles. Emotions run high. Celebs are exhausted, bruised, and under pressure to improve - not just for the judges, but for the millions watching at home. Some crumble. Some cry. Some even threaten to quit. But with the right partner and enough patience, breakthroughs happen.

And oh, the *breakthroughs*. That moment when it finally clicks - when the rhythm lands, the timing aligns, and suddenly they're dancing, really dancing - it's electric. I've seen seasoned pros tear up watching their partners nail a tricky paso for the first time. It's why they do it. It's why we watch.

Now, let's talk about the **rivalries** - because for all its sparkle, *Strictly* is still a competition. And while most of the cast cheer each other on, there's always a subtle undercurrent of comparison. Who's getting the better dance? Who's pulling higher scores? Who's being favoured in the edit?

Some rivalries are playful - cheeky side-eyes in group rehearsals, competitive banter in the green room. Others? Frostier. There's a famous tale of two celebs who were neck-and-neck in the leaderboard and refused to even rehearse in the same wing of the studio. One allegedly "borrowed" the other's hairspray just to ruffle feathers.

Even the pros aren't immune. They're fiercely proud of their work - and fiercely protective of their choreography. If one pro sees another borrowing a signature move, expect fireworks. But despite these tensions, there's a mutual respect that keeps things professional. Everyone knows the grind. Everyone respects the glitter game.

Then there's the **pro-to-celeb relationship** - part coach, part therapist, part best mate. Some pairings click instantly. Others... not so much. Clashes happen. One celeb dancer was famously booted from rehearsal for showing up late *every*day. The pro, at their wit's end, said, "You can learn the cha-cha on your own today." Harsh? Maybe. But it worked. They made it to the quarterfinals.

Some pros are strict and regimented - all counts, core, and clean lines. Others take a looser approach - encouraging flair, storytelling, even silliness. The magic is finding the right balance for each partnership. And when it works, the bond is unbreakable. Many celeb-pro pairs stay close long after the show ends, having forged a friendship through sweat, bruises, and ballroom glory.

Midweek, the couples head to **Elstree Studios** for camera blocking and stage rehearsals. This is where routines are polished for television - lighting cues refined, camera angles marked, entrances timed to the second. It's a rude awakening for some: what worked in a studio with mirrors doesn't always translate to a giant studio filled with lights, fog, and floor managers shouting instructions.

Tech day is also the first time couples see the *other* routines – and it's usually a reality check. "Oh god," you'll hear a celeb mutter, watching a rival nailing a 42-lift salsa with a grin. Cue panic. Cue imposter syndrome. Cue extra rehearsals until midnight.

Despite all this – the exhaustion, the injuries, the tears – there's a strange kind of joy in the grind. The *Strictly* rehearsal room becomes a crucible. Out of that pressure, something beautiful emerges: courage. Connection. Confidence. By Friday, the terrified rookie from Monday has become a performer. Not a pro, perhaps – but a dancer, nonetheless.

And when they finally step onto the studio floor Saturday night, in front of the cameras, judges, and that roaring audience – it's no longer just about the steps. It's about the story they've lived all week long.

And next? We leave the rehearsal sweat behind and step into the spotlight. It's live show time. From backstage nerves to standing ovations, let's take a spin through *Saturday Night Fever: The Strictly Live Show Experience...*

7

Saturday Night Fever – The Strictly Live Show Experience

Curtain Up – Lights, Cameras, and Last-Minute Nerves

The red light blinks. The band strikes up. Claudia and Tess strut down that iconic staircase. And just like that, we're live. For viewers at home, it's a glittery, glamorous two-hour spectacle. But behind the scenes? It's a military operation covered in rhinestones. Every beat, every step, every twirl must land perfectly - or at least convincingly - in real time.

Ask anyone involved, and they'll tell you: *Strictly* Saturdays don't begin at 6:30 PM. They begin *at dawn*. By 8:00 AM, hair and makeup is in full swing. The cast trickles in with coffee cups, script folders, and nerves jangling like chandelier earrings. Pros are stretching. Celebs are pacing. Wardrobe is on high alert. And the crew? Already fine-tuning lights, testing cameras, and running over cues for the tenth time.

The day is a blur of **run-throughs and tech checks**. Every performance is rehearsed again on the main stage - but now with lighting cues, live music, and cameras rolling. Directors watch every step through monitors, tweaking angles and deciding when to cut to the judges or pan across the floor. This is also the moment contestants realise: the real floor is *slippery*, the lights are *blinding*, and every misstep is one cough away from national humiliation.

By lunchtime, it's time for a **dress rehearsal** - a full run-through of the show with stand-in judges, a faux audience, and everything played as if it were the real thing. It's often hilariously chaotic. Someone misses their cue. Someone forgets their lines. The glitter cannon goes off two numbers early. It's a chance to iron out kinks, calm nerves, and work out whether Craig's judge's chair is still squeaking.

Afternoon turns to evening. The studio floor is cleared. The judges arrive, usually to warm welcomes from the crew (and the odd eye-roll depending on the mood). Tess and Claudia run lines with cue cards. The band does one last sound check. By now, the audience has begun to arrive - dressed to the nines and buzzing with anticipation. It's *Strictly* Saturday, and they've got the best seats in the house.

Backstage, the **energy shifts**. What was once nerves and bustle becomes something quieter. Focused. Serious. Celebrities retreat into themselves - pacing, breathing, whispering last-minute questions to their pros. "Do I spin after the lunge?" "What if I forget the timing?" "Remind me again what I do with my *arms*?"

The pros become coaches, cheerleaders, and part-time therapists. Some couples run steps in the corridors. Others meditate in corners. One pair I remember did a secret handshake every week – a private ritual to ground themselves before stepping into the spotlight.

Then it happens. The **floor manager gives the ten-minute call**. The lights dim. The audience erupts. Tess and Claudia step into place. The music starts. The show is live.

From here, everything moves *fast*. The opening number dazzles – a big group routine, sequins everywhere, the pros flying around like human glitterbombs. Once it's over, couples race backstage to change or prepare. The floor crew move like ghosts, silently repositioning props and scenery. Every single second is mapped, timed, and choreographed to within an inch of its life.

As each couple performs, **the pressure is immense** – but so is the support. Celebs dance their hearts out, knowing that for two minutes, the nation is watching. The crowd claps in time. The judges watch like hawks. The pros dance with both precision and protection – subtly guiding their partners if things go awry, always ready to cover a stumble with a smile.

And when it's over? Applause. Relief. Sometimes tears. A jog back up the stairs to Claudia's Corner, where Claudia Winkleman greets each couple like an eccentric fairy godmother with a clipboard. Her job isn't just to ask questions – it's to *ground* them. After the adrenaline of the dance, her warm words and knowing glances bring them gently back to Earth.

Then come the **judges' comments**. Ah yes – praise, puns, and the occasional dagger. Shirley waxes lyrical about posture. Craig raises a single eyebrow. Motsi bounces with joy. Anton charms with a twinkle in his eye. The scores flash up and the tension lifts – or drops, depending on how things went.

Between dances, the camera pans across the studio – sometimes catching pros whispering encouragement, celebs practicing steps, or a rogue glitterball swinging out of frame. Every moment is orchestrated to keep the pace brisk, the tension high, and the glamour at full wattage.

Backstage, it's a revolving door of wardrobe fixes, pep talks, and pep pills (figuratively speaking). Everyone's on high alert – dressers prepping costume changes, assistants adjusting microphones, producers whispering cues. It's organised chaos, held together by love, experience, and industrial-strength hairspray.

And when the final dance ends and the leaderboard is set? The entire cast gathers for that iconic group shot, clapping along to the credits while silently wondering – who's in the bottom two? Who's going home? What will the public decide?

But that's tomorrow's problem. For now, the glitter rains down. The credits roll. And the studio floor, for just a moment, becomes the most magical place on Earth.

Next, we head into the Sunday showdown – the dance-off, the drama, and the bittersweet farewells that come with elimination night.

The Sunday Show – Dance-Offs, Tears & the Glitterball Guillotine

If Saturday is a celebration, Sunday is a reckoning. The studio looks the same, the glitterball still glimmers, but the mood has shifted. There's tension in the air, heavy with the knowledge that by the end of the night, one couple's Strictly journey will end. And though the audience knows the results are pre-recorded on Saturday night, the emotions are no less real. For the dancers, the Sunday show is a cocktail of adrenaline, dread, and drama.

The day begins with an unusual kind of calm. The big performances are over. There are no all-day rehearsals, no fresh routines to perfect. Instead, there's waiting. Waiting for the votes. Waiting for the results. Waiting to find out who has danced their last paso. The cast gathers in the green room, making small talk that's anything but small. Who scored high enough to feel safe? Who's sweating bullets over a four from Craig? Nobody knows until the results are read.

When Tess and Claudia announce the first names through, relief floods the room. Couples cheer, hug, and breathe sighs so loud they could blow the glitter off a feathered skirt. But for those still waiting? Agony. As names are called, the tension builds. And then – silence. The dreaded announcement: "In the bottom two this week are..."

Cue gasps, cutaways to shocked faces, and sometimes, outright boos from the audience. Even after nearly twenty series, the reveal still has the power to shock. Big scorers sometimes tumble. Fan favourites fall. The voting public is unpredictable, and that unpredictability is part of the thrill.

Then comes the **dance-off** - Strictly's ultimate crucible. Two couples, one more chance. For the pros, it's an intense balancing act. They must keep their celeb calm, reframe the nerves, and deliver the routine of their lives, all while knowing the judges' eyes are sharper than ever. There's no room for mistakes. Every heel turn, every flick, every arm extension matters.

For celebs, it's brutal. They've already performed once. Their bodies are sore, their nerves frayed, their adrenaline drained. To muster the strength to dance again is nothing short of heroic. Some rise to the challenge - delivering cleaner, crisper, more powerful second performances. Others falter, nerves and fatigue clouding their steps.

And then the judges deliberate. It's usually tense, sometimes teary. Shirley will reference technique. Craig, ever the perfectionist, will cite "precision" or "timing." Motsi might lean into emotion and storytelling. Anton brings wit, warmth, and experience. And occasionally, they don't agree. Cue the drama of a split vote and the Head Judge's casting decision. One couple is saved. One couple goes home.

The eliminated pair then has their final moment - the **farewell dance**. It's often messy, more hugging than waltzing, but it's symbolic. A chance for closure. To thank their pro, their supporters, and the show that gave them sequins, spray tans, and memories to last a lifetime. Claudia, ever the comforter, offers kind words, tissues, and the occasional comedic aside to soften the blow.

What makes Sunday nights so compelling isn't just the drama

of elimination - it's the humanity. We see celebrities who, just weeks earlier, couldn't find the beat, now sobbing because they don't want the journey to end. We see pros comforting them, proud of their progress regardless of results. We see the camaraderie of the cast - rivals on the leaderboard, united in empathy when someone goes home.

And let's not forget the **group performances** that punctuate the Sunday shows. These pro-led spectacles often celebrate icons, eras, or themes - from Broadway medleys to heartfelt tributes. They're a reminder of the sheer artistry of the pros and a chance to showcase the show's magic without the pressure of competition.

There's also the **musical guest slots** - legends of the music industry gracing the Strictly stage. From Tony Bennett to Taylor Swift, Diana Ross to Ed Sheeran, the live performances add an extra layer of glamour. And who doesn't love watching the pros choreograph a dazzling routine around a superstar belting out a classic?

Yet, for all the razzle-dazzle, the heart of the Sunday show is always the elimination. It's bittersweet, poignant, and very, very Strictly. The journey ends for one, but continues for the rest - and with every departure, the competition sharpens. The glitterball gets closer. The stakes rise higher.

As the credits roll, hugs are exchanged, tears wiped, and promises made to reunite for the final. And while one couple heads home, the rest head straight back into the grind - Monday morning waits, and the next dance is already calling.

And so, the cycle continues. Saturday night glory, Sunday night heartbreak, and back to the rehearsal rooms on Monday. But next, let's raise the temperature - and the drama - with the phenomenon that turns Strictly from a TV show into a cultural event: *Theme Weeks*.

Themes, Thrills & the Power of a Paso in Fancy Dress

If *Strictly Come Dancing* is a feast, then the theme weeks are the extravagant desserts - over the top, sugary sweet, occasionally chaotic, but utterly irresistible. They're the moments when even the most sceptical viewer leans in and says, "Go on then, let's see what they do this week." And whether it's Movie Week, Halloween, or Musicals, these themed extravaganzas are where Strictly embraces its inner theatre kid, unashamedly camp and gloriously fun.

Let's start with **Movie Week**, a fan favourite and often the first theme of the series. Suddenly, celebs aren't just learning a dance - they're embodying a character. One week it's *Grease*, the next it's *The Lion King*. Outfits become costumes, choreography becomes storytelling, and the studio transforms into a Hollywood soundstage. Some of the most iconic Strictly routines have come from Movie Week - think Jay McGuiness and Aliona Vilani's *Pulp Fiction* jive, or Emma Barton channeling Audrey Hepburn in a dazzling foxtrot. Movie Week is where contestants stop being contestants and start being stars.

Then there's **Halloween Week**, Strictly's annual goth-glitter spectacular. Pumpkins, prosthetics, dry ice, and more cobwebs than a haunted mansion. The costumes are outrageous, the makeup team goes wild, and the dances often lean into the theatrical. A paso doble becomes a vampire showdown. A Charleston turns into a zombie romp. Sometimes it's terrifying, sometimes it's hilarious, but it's always unforgettable. Ed Balls' "Thriller" salsa is still whispered about in Strictly folklore - equal parts horrifying and brilliant.

And how could we forget **Musicals Week**? A West End spectacular in its own right, where every routine feels like a mini production. Pros and celebs step into the shoes of Broadway icons, performing to classics from *Les Misérables*, *Chicago*, *Cats*, and more. The staging is big, the vocals (from Strictly's live singers) are soaring, and the atmosphere is electric. For some celebs, this is their chance to indulge their inner showbiz dreams - and for the audience, it's pure spectacle.

But theme weeks aren't just about fun - they're about **testing versatility**. A waltz is one thing, but a waltz in full Shrek makeup while dressed as Princess Fiona? That takes a different kind of resilience. The costumes, props, and elaborate concepts often add layers of complexity to already difficult routines. Imagine trying to nail a quickstep while wearing a cape that keeps getting tangled around your ankles. Or maintaining paso intensity when your partner is dressed as a werewolf with fangs slipping mid-dance. It's challenging, absurd, and often hilarious.

These weeks also tap into the **shared cultural memory** of the audience. Everyone has a favourite film, a beloved musical, or a fondness for spooky season. When those cultural touchstones meet ballroom and Latin, magic happens. Families watch together, generations connect, and suddenly Strictly isn't just a competition - it's a national event.

Of course, with great spectacle comes great unpredictability. Theme weeks are notorious for producing **Strictly disasters**. Costumes that malfunction. Props that misbehave. One contestant famously tripped over a giant cane during Musicals Week and carried on dancing with it stuck to their foot for half the routine. Another was so distracted by the dry ice in Halloween Week that they missed an entire section of choreography. And yet, the audience loved them for it - because Strictly isn't about perfection. It's about effort, joy, and the ability to laugh through the glitter.

What makes these themed shows truly special is their ability to level the playing field. A celeb struggling with technique can suddenly shine if given a character to inhabit. Acting ability, charisma, and willingness to commit often matter more than perfect footwork. We've seen underdogs thrive in theme weeks, earning standing ovations not for textbook technique, but for sheer entertainment value.

At their best, theme weeks give us **iconic television moments**. Routines that are replayed for years, gifs shared on social media, watercooler conversations on Monday mornings. They're a reminder that Strictly is as much about joy and spectacle as it is about scoring tens.

And when the glitter settles, when the pumpkins are packed away and the Hollywood props wheeled off stage, the competition resumes - sharper, more intense, and with the stakes raised ever higher. Because every theme week is a reminder that Strictly is more than a dance show. It's theatre. It's television. It's Britain's Saturday night heartbeat.

Next, we'll step away from the sparkle for a moment and look into the people who decide the fate of the contestants week after week - the panel that sparks cheers, boos, and endless debates: the judges.

8

The Judges – Praise, Pouts & Paddle Drama

From Len to Shirley – The Evolution of the Panel

Every great show needs its heroes, its villains, and its storytellers. On *Strictly Come Dancing*, that role belongs to the judges. They're not just there to critique a heel turn or nit-pick a paso - they're characters in their own right. Beloved, loathed, cheered, and booed, the judges are as much a part of Strictly's DNA as the glitterball trophy itself. And like the dances, the panel has evolved, shifting with the times while keeping its own brand of drama intact.

When *Strictly* launched in 2004, its original judging lineup became instant icons. At the helm was **Len Goodman**, the Head Judge - a ballroom purist with a twinkle in his eye, a Kentish drawl, and a catchphrase that would echo through the ages: "Seven!" Len wasn't just a judge - he was the embodiment of Strictly's heart, a bridge between the old world of ballroom and the new world of Saturday night entertainment. His critiques were fair, his warmth genuine, and his authority unquestioned.

Alongside Len sat **Bruno Tonioli**, Strictly's resident fire-cracker. An Italian choreographer with more energy than a samba band on double espresso, Bruno turned judging into performance art. He leapt from his chair, flailed his arms, and described dances with metaphors so wild they sounded like poetry from another planet. Love him or roll your eyes, Bruno made every critique a spectacle.

Then there was **Craig Revel Horwood**, the pantomime villain we all secretly adore. With his sharp tongue, arch delivery, and infamous "It was a di-sas-ter, darling," Craig brought the grit to the glitter. He was harsh but often right, a stickler for technique who never sugar-coated his scores. Yet beneath the boos and gasps, audiences knew Craig's standards raised the bar. Without him, a ten wouldn't mean quite as much.

Completing the quartet was **Arlene Phillips**, a choreographer with decades of West End experience. Arlene brought both glamour and grit, offering detailed notes and championing performance as much as precision. Her departure after Series Six sparked debate, but her influence on Strictly's early years is undeniable.

As the years rolled on, the panel shifted. **Alesha Dixon** famously crossed the floor from contestant to judge, a move that divided audiences but reflected the show's willingness to evolve. Her warmth and relatability connected with viewers, even as purists longed for more technical critique. Later, **Darcey Bussell** joined, bringing Royal Ballet pedigree, elegance, and the kind of posture that could silence a room. She added grace and credibility, balancing Craig's bite with soft-spoken authority.

Today, the panel is led by **Shirley Ballas**, who stepped into Len's shoes as Head Judge in 2017. A decorated ballroom champion, Shirley brought technical depth and no-nonsense honesty. At first, viewers were divided, but over time, her warmth and steel have made her a mainstay. Alongside Shirley sit Craig (still arch, still sharp, still unmissable), and **Motsi Mabuse**, who burst onto the panel in 2019 with infectious energy, heartfelt passion, and a gift for connecting performance to emotion. Add in **Anton du Beke**, who swapped tails for a paddle after years as a pro, and the panel feels like a family - with just enough bickering to keep it spicy.

What makes the judges so compelling isn't just their critiques - it's their chemistry. Len rolling his eyes at Bruno's antics. Craig sparring with Shirley. Motsi bouncing in her chair while Anton delivers a dad joke. The panel are performers in their own right, and their interplay shapes the rhythm of every episode.

They also reflect the **bigger story of Strictly** - its balance between tradition and reinvention. Len's "old school" ballroom expertise anchored the show's roots. Shirley's leadership ensures the technical legacy endures. But Bruno, Motsi, and Anton bring flair, humour, and accessibility, reminding us that Strictly isn't just about heel leads and fleckerls - it's about joy.

The panel has had its controversies. Allegations of bias, accusations of harshness, fan campaigns demanding changes. But that's part of the theatre. The judges invite debate, fuel Monday morning office chatter, and keep Strictly firmly in the spotlight. Love them or loathe them, you can't ignore them.

And through it all, one thing remains constant: when those paddles come out, the nation holds its breath. Whether it's Craig's dreaded "2," Bruno's chaotic "10," or Len's iconic "SEVERN!", the scores are as much a part of Strictly as the dances themselves.

Next, we'll peek behind the polished critiques and glittering paddles to uncover the real dynamics of the panel - the feuds, the friendships, and the fiery debates that never quite make it to air.

Behind the Desk – Feuds, Friendships & the Politics of Judging

From the viewer's perspective, the judging panel is a row of sequinned sages dispensing wisdom and wit between dances. But behind that glossy desk lies a tangle of egos, allegiances, rivalries, and unspoken politics that have shaped Strictly's story as much as any samba or foxtrot.

Let's start with the most famous double act: **Len Goodman and Bruno Tonioli**. Their friendship spanned decades before *Strictly* and it showed. Where Len was measured, Bruno was manic; where Len sought balance, Bruno thrived in chaos. Their bickering was part Morecambe and Wise than mortal enemies, a comedic rhythm that audiences adored. Off-screen, they were lunch companions, gossip sharers, and fellow travellers between London and LA (*Dancing with the Stars* was their other gig). It was genuine camaraderie, sprinkled with rehearsed banter, and it kept the desk lively.

Then came **Craig Revel Horwood**, who always felt like the outsider at the desk - and thrived on it. His relationship with Len was fascinating. Len often bristled at Craig's relentless negativity, while Craig rolled his eyes at Len's more generous scoring. Yet over time, a mutual respect grew. Len knew Craig's standards raised the bar; Craig knew Len's warmth balanced the scales. Their sparring was real, but so was their respect.

The judges' lineup has never been immune to controversy. When **Alesha Dixon** joined the panel in 2009, many criticised the decision, claiming she lacked technical expertise. The backlash was intense, but her presence also highlighted an important question: should judges represent the audience's view as much as the professional critique? Alesha brought relatability, if not ballroom depth - and though short-lived, her tenure shifted the conversation about what a Strictly judge should be.

Darcey Bussell's addition in 2012 brought ballet elegance to the mix. At first, she struggled with live TV nerves - her critiques sometimes tentative, her voice soft against the bigger personalities. But her grace, kindness, and authority as a dancer eventually balanced the panel. She often played peacekeeper, smoothing Craig's edges or defusing Bruno's theatrics with a raised brow. When she left in 2018, it was with dignity and little drama - very Darcey.

Today, the panel is as dynamic as ever. **Shirley Ballas** arrived in 2017, stepping into Len's enormous shoes. Initially, she faced criticism for being "too harsh" or "too technical," but she soon won respect. Her rapport with Craig is particularly interesting. They often disagree - spectacularly so - with Craig nit-picking artistry while Shirley insists on technical merit. Their debates can feel heated, but insiders say it's all part of the Strictly dance: tension for TV, grounded in genuine respect for each other's expertise.

Then there's **Motsi Mabuse**, whose infectious energy and deep emotional connection to dance brought new life to the panel. Her warmth contrasts beautifully with Craig's frost. But her presence also raised eyebrows, as her sister Oti was still competing as a pro at the time. Producers insisted on fairness, and Motsi proved her professionalism by judging with both passion and impartiality. Still, her arrival revealed just how political the panel can feel to viewers - every relationship scrutinised, every word dissected.

And what of **Anton du Beke**? After years as the nation's favourite pro, his transition to judge was a moment of Strictly symmetry. He's the bridge between the dancefloor and the desk, with the authority of experience and the humour of someone who's been there, done that, and worn the sequins. He tends to play "Mr. Nice Guy," softening blows with wit, but that doesn't mean he won't call out sloppy technique when he sees it. His presence completes today's panel with warmth, knowledge, and a wink to long-time fans.

But let's not pretend it's all harmony and sequins. The **politics of judging** are real. Producers shape the narrative - encouraging judges to highlight certain story arcs, soft-pedal certain critiques, or hype up rivalries. Fans speculate endlessly about "favourite" contestants, "unfair" scoring, or behind-the-scenes bias. The truth is likely more nuanced: judges are human, with preferences, moods, and personal tastes that inevitably seep through.

And yet, that very unpredictability keeps Strictly alive. A Craig "1" can spark headlines. A Bruno "10" can cause outrage. Shirley's casting vote has reduced contestants to tears. The panel is theatre as much as adjudication - a place where feuds are fought, friendships forged, and politics played out in front of millions.

Still, when the music fades and the glitter settles, most judges insist the relationships are far warmer than the spats suggest. They bicker, they banter, they sometimes clash - but they share a love of dance and a devotion to the show. Off-camera, they're more likely to share a glass of wine than a cutting remark.

Next, we'll move from the personalities behind the paddles to the real heart of their role: how those numbers are chosen, what they really mean, and whether the judges' scores truly decide the fate of the glitterball.

Scoring the Sparkle – What the Numbers Really Mean

Few things in television inspire as much passion as four little paddles. The judges' scores on *Strictly Come Dancing* are more than numbers - they're cultural touchstones, shorthand for success or disaster. A "10" can feel like a coronation, a "4" like a public flogging. But behind those digits lies a fascinating system of tradition, performance, politics, and psychology.

Let's start with the basics. Each judge scores a performance from 1 to 10, based on their expertise, instincts, and (let's be honest) entertainment value. Add the four scores together, and you've got the judges' total. But here's the twist: those numbers don't directly decide who stays and who goes. Instead, they're converted into *rankings*, which are then combined with the public vote. This means the judges can influence, but not dictate, the outcome. It's democracy wrapped in sequins.

Still, the **weight of the scores** is enormous. Contestants live and die by those paddles. A Craig "3" can feel devastating – his low scores sting precisely because they're rare and deliberate. Conversely, a Bruno "10" (sometimes awarded for sheer enthusiasm rather than technical brilliance) can boost morale even if it doesn't impress purists. Len's "SEV-ERN" became so iconic that it was less a score and more a cultural meme, shouted at pub quizzes and office parties across Britain.

But how are those numbers *really* chosen? Judges insist they score based on **three pillars**: technique, performance, and progression. Technique covers the nitty-gritty – foot placement, posture, timing. Performance is about storytelling, energy, and charisma. Progression reflects the journey: has this celeb improved since week one? A shaky cha-cha in Week Two might score a six; the same routine in the quarterfinals would get a three.

Of course, this system isn't always transparent. Fans often accuse judges of **"inconsistent scoring."** Why did one celeb get an eight for a messy samba while another only scraped a six for a far cleaner foxtrot? The truth is, scoring is as much about instinct and impact as it is about spreadsheets. Sometimes a routine simply "lands" – the music, the costume, the charisma combine into magic, and the judges reward the moment, not just the mechanics.

Then there's the question of **strategic scoring.** Conspiracy theories abound: are judges nudged by producers to keep certain contestants in longer? Do they over-score weaker dancers to avoid embarrassing exits, or under-score favourites to "keep the competition open"? Officially, no. Unofficially, many admit the show thrives on drama, and "shock" scores fuel conversation. A Craig "2" or a surprise Shirley "10" makes headlines, sparks debate, and keeps Strictly in the public eye.

But perhaps the most intriguing part of scoring is its **emotional impact**. Celebs often say the scores mean more to them than the public vote. A harsh critique can shatter confidence; a string of nines can transform a nervous amateur into a budding star. Pro dancers, too, feel the pressure - their reputations are tied to those paddles. A low score isn't just a jab at their celeb; it's a critique of their choreography, teaching, and artistry.

And yet, the **numbers don't tell the whole story.** History proves you don't need tens to win. Contestants like Chris Hollins, who charmed the nation with his likeability rather than perfect technique, lifted the glitterball despite rarely topping the leaderboard. On the flip side, "ringers" - celebs with prior dance training - often score high but fail to capture the public's heart. The judges' numbers matter, but they don't guarantee glory.

Over time, certain scores have taken on **mythic status.** Craig's elusive "10" - withheld until he's absolutely convinced - is a badge of honour. Len's "seven" became so legendary that contestants begged for it. Shirley's "nine" signals near-perfection, but always leaves room for "just a little more." And Bruno's tendency to fall off his chair while flashing a paddle is entertainment in itself.

Scoring also reveals the **personalities of the panel.** Craig is stingy, technical, the eternal perfectionist. Motsi rewards energy and expression. Shirley anchors her scores in ballroom fundamentals. Anton, ever the pro's pro, considers musicality and effort as much as polish. Their differences keep the system dynamic - frustrating at times, but never dull.

So what do the numbers really mean? They're not absolutes. They're part feedback, part theatre, part psychology. They reflect not just what happened on the floor, but how it felt in the room. And ultimately, they're fuel - pushing celebs to work harder, sparking debates among fans, and shaping the Strictly journey week by week.

Next, we leave the desk and return to the glitter-soaked dance-floor, where partnerships are forged, tested, and transformed. Because behind every score, there's a story - and behind every story, there's a pair of dancers learning to trust each other under the pressure of the spotlight.

9

Partnerships, Pairings & the Chemistry of Dance

The Pairing Up – Matchmaking, Strictly Style

One of the most anticipated moments of any Strictly series isn't a dance, a score, or even a costume reveal. It's that first episode when Tess and Claudia gather the celebrities on the studio floor and announce: *"Your Strictly partner is..."* Cue gasps, cheers, awkward hugs, and sometimes the look of pure terror. Because in that moment, a celebrity's fate is sealed.

The partnerships are the lifeblood of Strictly. They're what makes the show more than just a competition. Each pairing is a story - about trust, transformation, sometimes friction, and often unexpected friendship. But how are these pairings made? It's not random, though the show likes to play it as though fate decides. In truth, it's a meticulous process of matchmaking behind the scenes.

Producers consider height first. Ballroom hold demands a certain alignment, and pairing a six-foot-two actor with a five-foot pro just doesn't work. Beyond height, they weigh personality, ability, and storylines. A nervous newsreader might be paired with a nurturing pro. A bold pop star could be matched with a fiery teacher who pushes them harder. Sometimes they aim for contrasts, sometimes for harmony – always for entertainment.

From the pros' perspective, that moment of reveal is nerve-wracking. They know who they *hope* for - someone with rhythm, charisma, or at least the ability to tell left from right. They also know who they're praying they don't get - the contestant with two left feet and a diary too packed for rehearsals. But the best pros find a way to make it work. Their job is to choreograph, teach, encourage, and sometimes babysit their celeb for up to three months.

The first days of rehearsal are crucial. That's when chemistry is built – or, in some cases, when cracks begin to show. A partnership with instant trust can soar, while one plagued by miscommunication can flounder, no matter how much talent is in the room. Some pairs click so completely they become iconic: think Jill Halfpenny and Darren Bennett, Kara Tointon and Artem Chigvintsev, or Rose Ayling-Ellis and Giovanni Pernice. These partnerships weren't just teacher and student - they were partnerships in the truest sense, two people meeting in the middle and creating something greater than the sum of their parts.

Of course, not every pairing is harmonious. The pressure cooker of Strictly can strain even the most patient personalities.

Exhaustion, nerves, and long rehearsal hours sometimes spark spats. Stories abound of celebs storming out, pros losing their temper, and both sides struggling to balance egos with effort. And yet, even difficult partnerships often produce compelling television – because friction, too, is part of the story.

What's remarkable is how often the partnerships transcend the dancefloor. Many Strictly pairs remain close long after their series ends. Some find lasting friendships. Others find romance. A few even find marriage. Strictly has given us wedded couples, Strictly babies, and more than a few tabloid scandals along the way. Love it or loathe it, the "Strictly Curse" is proof of how intense and intimate these partnerships can be.

For the audience, the partnerships are everything. They give us heroes to root for, journeys to follow, and stories that hook us week after week. Watching a nervous novice blossom under a pro's guidance is pure Strictly magic. Seeing two opposites learn to trust each other, laugh together, and eventually dazzle the judges – that's what keeps millions tuning in.

Because Strictly, at its heart, isn't just about steps and scores. It's about human connection. And nowhere is that more visible than in the partnerships – those glittering, flawed, funny, and sometimes fiery duos who step out onto the floor together and make us believe, just for a moment, that anything is possible with a little trust, a little rhythm, and a lot of sequins.

Next, we'll look deeper into what happens once the music starts – how partnerships evolve under the pressures of training, how trust is tested, and how chemistry (or the lack of it) plays out on the dancefloor.

Trust, Tiffs & Tango Tensions

If the first week of Strictly partnerships feels like a blind date - all smiles, compliments, and cautious optimism - then the following weeks are more like a marriage under a spotlight. The reality sets in: hours of gruelling rehearsals, bruised toes, missed steps, and the relentless countdown to Saturday night. This is where the true test of trust begins, and where sparks - of every kind - tend to fly.

At its best, the partnership becomes a cocoon of support. Celebs lean on their pros for more than choreography. They need encouragement, patience, and the occasional pep talk when self-doubt creeps in. For some, those rehearsal rooms become sanctuaries, places where they can fail, cry, laugh, and try again without judgement. But at its worst, that same intensity can strain even the brightest partnerships.

One former contestant admitted, "You're together more than you're with your own family. You're tired, you're stressed, and you're being asked to do something you've never done before in front of millions. Of course there are arguments." And argue they do. Pros push hard because they know what's at stake. Celebs sometimes push back, frustrated by sore bodies or fragile confidence. A tense rehearsal spat might blow over with a laugh, or linger long enough to affect the week's performance.

The **trust dynamic** is fascinating. Ballroom and Latin are built on physical trust. A celebrity has to literally let themselves be led, lifted, spun, and sometimes dropped into the arms of their pro. That doesn't happen overnight. It takes weeks of missteps, reassurance, and small victories. When trust builds, routines soar. When it cracks, the nerves show on the dancefloor.

Consider the lifts in a salsa or American smooth. For a pro, they're second nature. For a celeb, they're terrifying. To commit to being hoisted into the air - and trust your partner not to let you crash - requires a leap of faith. When it works, the audience gasps in delight. When it doesn't... well, that's when Strictly's infamous blooper reels are born.

Of course, not all tension is negative. Sometimes, a bit of **friction fuels brilliance**. The most competitive celebs thrive on being pushed, even if it means butting heads. A fiery rehearsal can produce electrifying paso dobles or sambas bursting with energy. In these cases, tension becomes chemistry, and chemistry becomes performance gold.

But there are moments when tension spills over. Tabloids love to pounce on stories of celebs storming out of rehearsals or pros losing patience. While many of these tales are exaggerated, the kernel of truth is this: Strictly partnerships are intense, high-pressure bonds. And intensity, by nature, breeds drama.

Yet what keeps these duos going isn't perfection - it's resilience. Again and again, celebs describe the moment when they nearly gave up... and their pro pulled them back. A tough love speech, a small breakthrough, a shared laugh at a spectacular mistake - these are the turning points where partnerships either crumble or deepen.

It's no wonder the "Strictly Curse" looms so large in the public imagination. These partnerships are deeply intimate. Hours of physical closeness, emotional vulnerability, and mutual reliance can blur lines between professional and personal. For some, it ends in scandal. For others, it's simply the price of creating something authentic together.

Audiences pick up on these dynamics instinctively. A partnership that feels fractured makes viewers uneasy. One that radiates trust and joy pulls people in, week after week. It's why some couples become "fan favourites" regardless of technical skill - because their relationship tells a story we all want to follow.

And when the trust is real, it shows. You see it in the way a celeb looks at their pro before the music starts, in the shared grin after a perfect spin, in the embrace at the end of a routine. These moments remind us that Strictly isn't just about steps. It's about human connection - fragile, messy, and glorious in equal measure.

Next, we'll see how those connections translate into performance - the unspoken electricity between two people moving in sync, and the moments where chemistry itself becomes the secret weapon of a winning dance.

When Chemistry Becomes Magic - The Partnerships That Defined Strictly

Every Strictly season has its frontrunners, its underdogs, and its comic relief. But every so often, a partnership emerges that transcends the competition. Two people who find such ease, joy, and electricity in their dancing together that the audience forgets about the scores, the judges, and even the glitter. These partnerships are where Strictly becomes more than a TV show. They become part of cultural memory.

Take **Jill Halfpenny and Darren Bennett** in Series Two. Jill was a soap star with confidence, Darren a new pro eager to prove himself. From the first paso to their now-legendary jive, they crackled with energy. Jill's talent was obvious, but it was the chemistry between the two that made them unmissable. They weren't just dancing – they were sparking off each other, feeding each other's energy, building routines that felt alive. Their final jive still gets replayed as one of the greatest Strictly moments of all time.

Or consider **Rose Ayling-Ellis and Giovanni Pernice**. Rose, the show's first deaf contestant, faced challenges no other celeb had encountered. Giovanni, a passionate, fiery pro, adjusted his entire teaching style to meet her needs. The result wasn't just brilliant dancing – it was a groundbreaking partnership built on mutual respect, patience, and creativity. Their Couple's Choice routine, with a section performed in silence to represent Rose's world, became a defining moment for Strictly and won a BAFTA. More than chemistry, it was empathy, trust, and artistry combined.

Then there's the charm of **Chris Hollins and Ola Jordan**, proof that you don't need to be the best dancer to win. Their partnership was pure joy. Chris wasn't the most technical, but his enthusiasm was infectious. Ola coaxed out performances full of humour and heart, and their easy friendship made them a fan favourite. They proved that chemistry isn't about perfection – it's about connection, and the audience could feel it.

Of course, Strictly has also had its **romantic sparks**. Kara Tointon and Artem Chigvintsev's 2010 partnership turned into a real-life love story. Their chemistry was undeniable on the dancefloor – every rumba smouldered, every waltz glowed.

Viewers were hooked not just on their routines, but on the will-they-won't-they tension that simmered week after week. It was romance told through dance, and it felt authentic because it *was*.

Not all magical partnerships are about winning. Sometimes it's the surprise journeys that captivate. **Ed Balls and Katya Jones** were never destined for the glitterball, but their unlikely bond created TV gold. Ed threw himself into every routine with abandon, and Katya choreographed with wit and flair. Their "Gangnam Style" salsa might not have been technically brilliant, but it was joyous, ridiculous, and unforgettable. Chemistry, in their case, meant fun - and that too is Strictly magic.

What makes these partnerships shine isn't just the steps. It's the storytelling. When two people genuinely connect, it radiates through every lift and spin. Audiences at home don't just watch the dances - they invest in the relationship. We cheer their triumphs, groan at their stumbles, and cry when their journeys end. Strictly becomes a mirror of life itself: messy, emotional, sometimes hilarious, sometimes moving, but always about people finding connection.

The pros know this, too. They often say that the best partnerships aren't about skill, but about heart. A celeb who trusts their pro, listens, and embraces the joy of dance will create something more memorable than a technically perfect performance without connection. That's why the show continues to resonate after two decades - it's not just a contest, it's a collection of love stories, friendships, and partnerships that inspire us to believe in human connection.

And when chemistry truly becomes magic, the dancefloor transforms. The audience leans forward. The judges fall silent. And for a few minutes, Britain watches two people move as one, caught in a glittering moment that feels timeless. That's the Strictly effect - and it's why the partnerships are always at the heart of the show.

Next, we'll turn our gaze to the wider Strictly universe - not just the couples, but the fans who vote, cheer, and make the show a national treasure. Because what's Strictly without its audience?

10

The Fans – From Sofa Judges to Glitterball Devotees

Strictly Fever – How Britain Fell in Love with the Glitterball

Strictly is a show built on sequins, samba, and showbiz sparkle - but its true power lies in its audience. From the very first series in 2004, viewers didn't just watch; they invested. They became armchair critics, loyal supporters, and passionate voters. Strictly isn't just a programme that airs on Saturday nights - it's a national ritual, one that brings families together and sparks debates from living rooms to office watercoolers.

So why did Britain fall so hard for the glitterball? Part of it is nostalgia. Strictly resurrected ballroom and Latin at a time when they felt old-fashioned, almost forgotten. Suddenly, waltzes and tangos were back in vogue, but with a fresh, glamorous twist. For older generations, it rekindled memories of *Come Dancing*. For younger ones, it was brand-new, dazzling, and surprisingly addictive.

Another reason lies in Strictly's perfect balance of **competition and entertainment**. Unlike sport, the stakes are glittering rather than brutal. Unlike pure reality TV, the talent is real, the effort authentic. The show offers just enough jeopardy to keep us hooked, but wraps it in warmth and humour. It's competitive, yes – but it's also comforting. In a fractured world, Strictly is a safe space where the biggest drama is whether Craig will give a six or a seven.

And then there's the **ritual of the vote.** For fans, voting isn't just about supporting a favourite – it's about participation. You're not just a viewer; you're part of the story. Every phone call, every online click is a chance to keep your couple in, to play your part in the glittering drama. It's democracy sequinned, and it gives fans a sense of ownership over the show.

Over time, Strictly fans have become a culture of their own. There are the **sofa judges**, arms folded, ready to deliver their own critiques before the real panel chimes in. ("Too much gapping on the quickstep," mutters your aunt, who hasn't danced since primary school.) There are the **glitterball devotees**, who watch every interview, follow every pro on Instagram, and know the history of every Charleston ever danced. And then there are the **casual viewers**, tuning in for the sparkle, the music, and the chance to see their favourite soap star stumble through a salsa.

Fan culture also thrives on **debate.** Every Sunday, Twitter (or X, as it now calls itself) explodes with outrage, joy, and analysis. Was that a fair score? Should they have been in the dance-off? Is there a "fix"? Strictly thrives on this chatter, because the passion of its fans keeps it relevant and buzzing long after the glitter has settled on the studio floor.

And then there are the live audiences. Tickets are like gold dust, snapped up months in advance. For those lucky enough to sit in Elstree Studios on a Saturday night, it's an unforgettable experience. You're part of the magic – clapping, cheering, gasping, and even getting sprayed with the odd sequin. Fans who've attended say the atmosphere is electric, the scale of the production staggering, and the thrill of seeing those routines up close almost overwhelming.

What's remarkable is how **intergenerational** Strictly's fanbase is. Grandparents watch with grandchildren, families bond over favourite couples, friends debate who deserves the glitterball. Few shows can unite so many age groups, backgrounds, and tastes. Strictly is truly national in its appeal – a shared experience that transcends demographics.

Case studies from fans show how deeply the programme has embedded itself into British life. One family I spoke to times their Sunday dinner around the results show, complete with their own makeshift paddles for scoring. Another group of university students hold Strictly nights, complete with prosecco, glitter makeup, and sweepstakes. For both, Strictly isn't just TV – it's tradition.

Strictly fever doesn't stop at the UK's borders either. The format has gone global, with versions from *Dancing with the Stars* in the US to *Bailando por un Sueño* in Latin America. But British fans pride themselves on the original, the purest blend of ballroom and Saturday night showbiz.

What's clear is that the fans are the heartbeat of Strictly. They cheer, they vote, they debate, they obsess. Without them, the glitterball would be just a trophy. With them, it's a symbol of joy, unity, and national obsession.

Next, we'll step into the world of the superfans – those who go beyond voting and watching, who immerse themselves in every tour, spin-off, and gossip column, and whose dedication keeps the Strictly flame burning bright year-round.

Superfans, Spoilers & the Strictly Community

Every television show has its loyal viewers, but Strictly has something more: an army of superfans who breathe sequins, dream paso dobles, and mark their calendars around the glitterball. For these fans, Strictly isn't just a Saturday night treat – it's a lifestyle, a passion, and in some cases, an identity.

Let's start with the **spoiler hunters.** Because the results show is filmed on Saturday and aired on Sunday, the outcome is technically "secret" for 24 hours. But superfans know where to look. Forums, Twitter feeds, and carefully worded gossip posts share the leaked eliminations before Tess has even changed her gown. For some, knowing the result early is part of the thrill. For others, it's sacrilege. The spoiler wars are a Strictly fandom tradition, with arguments raging every year about whether leaks ruin or enrich the experience.

Then there are the **tour devotees.** Once the glitter settles at Elstree, Strictly takes to the road. The live tour is a phenomenon in its own right, with arenas across the UK filled with thousands of fans screaming for their favourite couples. Superfans follow the tour from city to city, making banners, meeting pros at stage doors, and even replicating costumes. For them, Strictly isn't just something you watch - it's something you chase.

Superfans also thrive in the world of **merchandise and memorabilia.** From sequinned cushions to official glitterball ornaments, the Strictly brand has found its way into homes across Britain. Online communities trade signed programmes, rare costumes, and behind-the-scenes souvenirs. To some, a glove once worn by Anton du Beke is a prized possession worthy of display.

And then there's the **Strictly community itself.** Online groups buzz year-round with discussions, throwbacks, and debates. Facebook pages dedicated to "Bring Back the Argentine Tango" or "Justice for the Jive" gather thousands. Reddit threads analyse choreography frame by frame. Instagram reels celebrate the best lifts, while TikTok is filled with fans recreating routines in their living rooms. In these spaces, friendships are forged, rivalries played out, and Strictly becomes more than a show - it becomes a shared language.

What's particularly striking about Strictly's superfans is their **creativity.** They don't just consume - they contribute. Fan art, parody accounts, podcasts, blogs, and fantasy leagues all add layers to the Strictly universe. Some design their own scoring apps. Others create fantasy casts, speculating months ahead about which celebs might sign up. The speculation is often as exciting as the show itself.

Superfan dedication has also produced some truly touching stories. One woman I spoke to said she watched every episode with her mother, who was battling illness. When her mother passed, she kept the tradition alive, hosting Strictly nights in her honour. Another fan found her closest friends through an online group, meeting up at live shows and travelling across the country together. For many, Strictly isn't just sparkle on the screen - it's comfort, community, and connection in the real world.

Of course, the passion sometimes boils over into controversy. Judges are accused of bias, pros of unfair choreography, celebs of getting "sympathy votes." Superfans argue passionately, sometimes viciously, about their favourites. And yet, this intensity proves how deeply people care. Strictly matters - not just as a show, but as a national talking point, a cultural cornerstone, a glitter-covered battleground.

What makes all of this so remarkable is that Strictly has managed to inspire such devotion without cynicism. Unlike many reality shows, its fanbase isn't built on cruelty or scandal. It's built on joy. Superfans may bicker about scores or spoilers, but at the heart of it, they love dance, they love performance, and they love the way Strictly makes them feel.

Next, we'll turn to a slightly different kind of fan - the **celebrity fans**, alumni, and ambassadors who keep Strictly's legacy alive beyond the show. Because once you've danced beneath that glitterball, Strictly never quite leaves you.

Beyond the Ballroom – Alumni, Ambassadors & Lifelong Fans

Strictly has always been more than just a television show. For many of its celebrities, pros, and even viewers, it becomes part of their identity – a glittering badge of honour they wear proudly long after their season ends. The alumni, ambassadors, and lifelong fans keep Strictly alive between series, ensuring its influence stretches far beyond the Saturday night slot.

Let's begin with the **alumni – the celebrities who danced once and never really left.** Many past contestants become ambassadors for the show, appearing on spin-offs like *It Takes Two*, cheering from the audience, or popping up for anniversary specials. Some, like Ore Oduba or Stacey Dooley, went on to reinvent their careers after their Strictly stints, moving into presenting and broadcasting with the confidence Strictly gave them. Winning the glitterball isn't just a trophy; for many, it's a launching pad.

Then there are the contestants who didn't win but still became part of the Strictly family. Think of Ed Balls, forever remembered for his joyful, gangly salsa. Or Ann Widdecombe, whose comedic turns made her a national talking point. These alumni may not be technical champions, but they embody Strictly's spirit – throwing themselves into dance and entertainment with gusto. Fans never forget them, and they, in turn, remain grateful to the show that gave them their moment in sequins.

The **professional dancers** are alumni in their own right too. When a pro retires, they don't simply vanish. Many stay connected through guest appearances, tours, or choreography roles. Some, like Ian Waite and Camilla Dallerup, became fixtures on *It Takes Two*, offering expert analysis. Others, like Pasha Kovalev and Flavia Cacace, launched stage shows, taking the Strictly brand to theatres across the country. The pros carry Strictly with them into every paso and pirouette they perform beyond the show.

Then there's the unique category of **celebrity superfans.** Actors, comedians, and even politicians have declared their love for Strictly. Some appear on the companion shows, while others join the audience with visible glee. The programme has a way of uniting unlikely admirers - from Dame Judi Dench, who once admitted she never misses an episode, to footballers who confessed to voting religiously. Strictly's reach extends into circles far removed from the ballroom, proving its universal appeal.

But perhaps the most enduring group are the **lifelong fans.** These are people who build traditions around Strictly, integrating it into the rhythm of their lives. They attend tours, buy DVDs of past seasons, and mark anniversaries of iconic dances. Some even take up ballroom classes themselves, inspired by watching celebrities learn. For many, Strictly sparks a love of dance that changes their lives. Studios across the UK report surges in sign-ups after each series, especially among older adults rediscovering the joy of movement.

Case studies show how profound this influence can be. One retired couple I spoke to started ballroom lessons after watching Rose and Giovanni. A year later, they'd lost weight, made friends, and found new joy in their retirement. Another fan, a teenager who once watched with her grandmother, went on to train as a professional dancer. Strictly was her gateway to a lifelong passion.

The legacy of alumni and ambassadors is also crucial for the show's survival. Each year, Strictly's reputation is bolstered by the stories of those who came before. When new celebs sign up, they often cite past contestants as their inspiration. "I saw so-and-so do it, and I thought - maybe I could too." The alumni network is part cheer squad, part proof of concept, and part glitterball-shaped family tree.

And in the end, whether you danced on that stage, choreographed behind the scenes, or voted from your sofa, being part of the Strictly community is something you carry with you. It lingers in memories of routines, in friendships formed, and in the way it made you feel on a cold winter's Saturday night when, for a couple of hours, the world sparkled a little brighter.

Next, we'll shift from the audience back into the heart of the show - the stagecraft itself. Because while the fans cheer and the alumni reminisce, Strictly's magic is made by an army behind the curtain, conjuring the sequinned spectacle every week.

11

Behind the Scenes – Sequins, Sweat & Stagecraft

The Hidden Army of Strictly

When millions of us tune in to Strictly on a Saturday night, we see the sparkle, the sequins, the smiles, and the smooth live production that feels almost effortless. But like any great performance, what happens on the surface is only the tip of the iceberg. Behind every waltz, every paso, and every glitter-soaked group number lies an army of people whose work is largely invisible but absolutely vital. Strictly isn't just a television programme - it's a logistical miracle brought to life each week by a team as large and complex as a West End production.

Let's start with the **wardrobe department**, which is practically a legend in its own right. The dresses, the tails, the feathers, the rhinestones - they don't just appear overnight. Each costume is hand-designed, tailored, and fitted to the celebrity and professional within days, sometimes hours, of the dance style being confirmed. Vicky Gill, head of costume, and her team are magicians who balance glamour with practicality. A dress must shimmer under the lights but also withstand spins, kicks, and frantic quickstep footwork. Sequins must be sewn so they don't fly off mid-routine; hems must be perfect to avoid tripping. Every week, dozens of costumes are built from scratch. It's a feat that would challenge even the most seasoned fashion house, yet they pull it off week after week. Celebs often say the first time they step into their Strictly costume, they *become* their character for the dance. That's the wardrobe's true magic - not just clothes, but transformation.

Then there's the **makeup and hair team**, another army in itself. Their remit isn't just making people look pretty; it's theatre on a scale rarely seen in live TV. From glitter-sprayed hair to dramatic smoky eyes, from false lashes that can be seen in the back row to wigs and extensions worthy of the West End, the team creates looks that match each routine's mood. One week, a celeb might need elegant 1920s waves for a foxtrot. The next, they're transformed into a neon pop diva for a cha-cha. And all of it must be done in record time. Contestants often describe quick changes between dances where hairpieces are yanked off, wigs pinned on, and makeup retouched in under five minutes. It's chaos, but it's Strictly chaos - and the results always shine.

Of course, none of this would matter without the **production crew.** These are the people who build the set, hang the lights, operate the cameras, and ensure that every angle of a lift is captured for the audience at home. Elstree Studios becomes a small city every Saturday, buzzing with technicians, runners, floor managers, and stagehands. Each camera shot is chore-ographed almost as tightly as the dances themselves. There's a plan for when to swoop across the floor, when to zoom in on a trembling hand, when to pan to the judges' faces. It's a ballet of technology that makes the at-home experience seamless. The live element adds extra pressure. With no room for error, a mistimed cue or a dropped camera shot could ruin a routine. And yet, week after week, it all runs like clockwork.

Then there's the **music department,** led by the Strictly band. This isn't background noise - it's one of the defining elements of the show. Unlike many versions of *Dancing with the Stars* worldwide, the BBC insisted from the start that Strictly would use live music. That means every samba beat, every waltz melody, every paso drumroll is performed live as the couples dance. The band rehearses relentlessly to capture the energy of the original songs while adapting them for dance. Vocalists, too, are unsung heroes - their voices soar through everything from Lady Gaga hits to classic Frank Sinatra ballads, often switching styles at breakneck speed within a single show. The result? A musical experience that feels alive, raw, and uniquely Strictly.

But perhaps the most fascinating backstage figures are the **choreographers and creative directors.** While pros design their weekly dances, the big showstoppers - group numbers, pro dances, specials - are masterminded by the creative team. Jason Gilkison, Strictly's longtime director of choreography, is responsible for turning the dancefloor into a different world each week. One week it's a Parisian café, the next a Broadway stage, the next a gothic ballroom filled with dry ice. These numbers are mini-productions in themselves, complete with props, set changes, and dozens of dancers. They showcase the pros' skills, yes, but they also keep the programme fresh and exciting. Fans may tune in for the celeb dances, but it's the pro group routines that often go viral the next morning.

And let's not forget the **floor runners, coordinators, and stage managers.** These unsung heroes keep the machine turning. They're the ones ushering celebs to the floor, calming nerves, handling last-minute costume tears, and making sure everyone is where they need to be. They're invisible to the viewer, but to the celebs, they're lifelines. One former contestant said, "The runners saved me every week. They gave me water, fixed my mic, and told me to breathe when I thought I was going to faint." It's these little human touches that keep the show from falling into chaos.

All of these moving parts come together under the **producers' watchful eyes.** Their role is to shape the story of Strictly each week. Who gets the "journey" edit? Which partnership is the focus of the pre-dance VT? How do you balance tension with fun? Producers pull the strings to ensure each episode has rhythm, pacing, and drama. They also have to be ready for anything. Wardrobe malfunctions, forgotten steps, even falls - all must be managed live, with minimal disruption.

Perhaps the most remarkable thing about Strictly's hidden army is how much they care. Time and again, celebrities remark on the sense of family behind the scenes. Yes, it's gruelling. Yes, it's stressful. But there's also camaraderie, laughter, and pride. From the seamstress sewing sequins at 2 a.m. to the lighting technician perfecting a spotlight, everyone knows they're part of something special.

And when the glitterball shines on a Saturday night, when the band swells, the costumes shimmer, and the celebs take to the floor, all of that invisible labour crystallises into a spectacle that feels effortless. That's the paradox of Strictly's hidden army: they work harder than anyone else, so that all we see is the magic.

Next, we'll take you even deeper into this backstage world - exploring the pressure, the last-minute dramas, and the extraordinary teamwork that turns chaos into choreography every single week.

Chaos & Choreography – Backstage on Show Night

Strictly may look like smooth, polished magic to the millions watching at home, but backstage on show night is a very different story. It's a world of nerves, noise, quick changes, and barely controlled chaos. The irony is that this chaos is not a flaw - it's part of the design. Out of the whirlwind comes the glamour, out of the panic comes the polish. To step backstage at Strictly is to step into organised mayhem, a glitter-soaked symphony of people pulling together to make live television look effortless.

The day begins long before Tess and Claudia step out under the spotlights. Saturday mornings at Elstree are a hive of activity. Contestants arrive with suitcases, garment bags, and half-finished cups of coffee. Some look buzzing with adrenaline, others bleary-eyed from late-night rehearsals. The pros are already running choreography one last time, drilling lifts in corners, checking spacing on the dancefloor. Hair and makeup are underway by mid-morning, with contestants being ferried in and out of chairs like a production line in sequins. One celebrity described it as "a beauty salon on steroids" - curling tongs, hairspray, and glitter everywhere, punctuated by cries of "Five minutes, darling, you're needed for rehearsal!"

The **dress run** is where the first real taste of chaos kicks in. It's the only full rehearsal with costumes, cameras, and the live band. Inevitably, something goes wrong. A hem rips. A lift fails. A mic pack slips mid-spin. This is where the floor managers earn their stripes, darting across the set to fix disasters before the cameras roll for real. Sometimes contestants crumble under the pressure of the dress run, leaving everyone worried. Other times, they save their best for the live show, proving the old adage: a bad dress rehearsal means a good performance.

As the afternoon edges into evening, tension thickens. Celebs pace backstage, muttering steps under their breath. Pros pump them up with pep talks or try to calm them with jokes. The green room buzzes with nervous chatter. Producers flit between contestants, reminding them of their VT intros, encouraging big smiles, warning against looking at the wrong camera. Every move is choreographed, not just the dances.

When the clock ticks down to showtime, the atmosphere shifts. Backstage corridors become rivers of sequins. Contestants line up for their entrances, the heat of the lights leaking through the curtain. One by one, they're ushered into place by runners with headsets, who whisper last-minute instructions. Then, with a swell of music, the magic begins. From the audience's perspective, it's smooth, glamorous. From backstage, it's like being in the middle of a hurricane.

During the live show, the **quick changes** are legendary. A celebrity might go from a ballroom gown to a salsa outfit in under five minutes. Behind the scenes, assistants rip Velcro fastenings, swap shoes, pin wigs, and glue on false eyelashes while floor managers shout countdowns: "Three minutes! Two minutes!" Contestants have described emerging onto the dancefloor still catching their breath, half-held together by pins and tape. And yet, to the viewer, they look flawless.

The **band and singers** add another layer to the chaos. Every song is live, meaning no two weeks are the same. Singers often juggle multiple numbers, shifting from soulful ballads to disco hits within minutes. A missed cue could throw off the entire performance, yet their professionalism means it rarely happens. Meanwhile, the sound engineers backstage work feverishly to balance vocals, instruments, and floor noise. It's live theatre wrapped inside live TV, with no safety net.

And then there are the **unexpected dramas.** Shoes snap. A light fizzles out. A celebrity forgets the steps halfway through a routine. Once, a prop collapsed on set during a live show, sending crew scrambling out of view of the cameras. Another time, a celeb fainted from nerves minutes before their dance, only to be revived, reassured, and pushed gently onto the floor with a smile plastered on. Strictly's motto could well be: "The show must go on – and it will, no matter what."

The **judges' desk** is its own hub of backstage tension. Between routines, producers feed them notes, nudging storylines along: highlight improvement here, point out posture there, keep the rivalry alive between two couples. Craig may scowl and Bruno may leap from his chair, but behind the desk are stacks of notes, coffee cups, and producers whispering in earpieces to make sure the narrative flows as smoothly as the cha-cha.

For the contestants, the wait to dance is agonising. Some prefer to watch from the sidelines, cheering on their fellow celebs. Others hide in the corridors, unable to look until it's their turn. One pro dancer once confessed: "The worst part isn't dancing. It's standing there in the tunnel, waiting for Tess to call your name. Your heart feels like it's going to leap out of your costume."

When the final credits roll, the chaos doesn't end. The audience heads home, but the crew stay late into the night, clearing costumes, dismantling sets, and prepping for Sunday's results show. Celebs and pros, buzzing with adrenaline, mingle backstage, some elated, some tearful. There are hugs, champagne toasts, and sometimes arguments. For the crew, it's straight into planning the next week - because in just a few days, the cycle starts all over again.

What's extraordinary is that, despite the frenzy, the finished product feels seamless. The quick changes, the missed cues, the panic attacks - none of it shows to the millions watching. That's the triumph of Strictly's backstage army: they take the chaos, choreograph it, and present us with magic. It's not that disaster doesn't happen - it's that the viewer never sees it.

Backstage at Strictly is not just about logistics; it's about people working together under extraordinary pressure. It's camaraderie forged in sequins and sweat, a shared mission to keep the glitterball turning. Celebs often say they leave Strictly not just with dance skills but with deep gratitude for the unseen crew who carried them through.

And so, while the ballroom shines brightest on screen, the true miracle of Strictly happens in the shadows – in the wings, the dressing rooms, and the corridors where chaos reigns, only to be spun into choreography week after week.

Next, we'll look at how this invisible machine manages to adapt, reinvent, and refresh itself year after year, keeping Strictly feeling new while never losing its core sparkle.

Reinventing the Glitterball – How Strictly Stays Fresh Year After Year

Strictly has been waltzing across British screens for two decades, a remarkable feat in a world where TV shows often burn brightly and then vanish within a few years. The question many ask is: how does it stay fresh? How has it kept audiences returning year after year, glued to their sofas every Saturday night, even in an age of streaming and on-demand? The secret lies not in a single trick, but in a delicate balance of reinvention and tradition – a glitterball that spins forward while never losing its shine.

First, let's talk about the **format itself.** At its heart, Strictly hasn't changed much since 2004. Celebrities are paired with professional dancers, they train all week, perform live, are scored by judges, and face elimination through a mix of scoring and public vote. That core structure is the show's anchor. Audiences know what they're getting: sparkle, dance, drama, and joy. Yet within that familiar framework, the show's producers constantly adjust the details. New dances are introduced (the Charleston, the Argentine Tango, Couple's Choice), keeping the repertoire fresh. Themes like Movie Week or Musicals Week are reinvented each year, offering new creative possibilities. And the special episodes - Halloween, Blackpool, Christmas - have become beloved fixtures that fans anticipate all season.

Then there's the **casting.** Strictly has mastered the art of variety. Each year's line-up balances different types of celebrity: the young pop star, the older actor, the athlete, the newsreader, the reality TV wildcard. This mix guarantees appeal across generations. It also ensures that every viewer has someone to root for - and someone to grumble about. Over time, the show has broadened its reach by embracing more diverse line-ups, including same-sex pairings, older contestants, and celebrities with disabilities. These decisions aren't just tokenistic - they're cultural milestones, proving Strictly can evolve with the times while staying true to its central promise: that anyone can dance.

The **judging panel** has also evolved strategically. When Len Goodman left, many feared the show would lose its centre. Instead, Shirley Ballas stepped in with her own style of authority, balancing Craig's sharp critiques and Bruno's exuberance. Later, Motsi Mabuse brought infectious warmth and Anton du Beke offered the pro's perspective from the other side of the desk. Each change refreshed the dynamic without alienating long-term fans. The judges are as much characters in the Strictly drama as the contestants - and rotating them carefully has kept the show's storytelling lively.

Behind the scenes, **production values** have risen dramatically.

The lighting rigs, camera work, and set designs grow more ambitious each year. Group numbers look like West End spectacles, with elaborate staging that would have been impossible in the early series. Technology plays its part too: AR graphics, sweeping Steadicam shots, and improved sound design make the show look fresher than ever, without losing the warmth of its live, human feel.

Another secret weapon is the **pro dancers themselves.** Strictly constantly renews its pro lineup, introducing fresh talent from around the world. Each new pro brings different influences - fiery Latin flair, contemporary theatricality, or classic ballroom precision. Their presence reinvigorates the choreography, pushing the show into new creative directions. At the same time, the long-standing pros provide continuity, beloved figures audiences look forward to each year. The balance between familiar faces and exciting newcomers keeps the pro cast dynamic.

Strictly has also embraced **cultural relevance.** The show is careful to reflect the wider world in subtle ways. Song choices, themes, and stories often connect with what's happening beyond the dancefloor. Rose Ayling-Ellis's silent section in her Couple's Choice routine became a national moment, sparking conversations about accessibility and representation. Similarly, the inclusion of same-sex pairings sent a powerful message of inclusivity, handled with warmth rather than sensationalism. By weaving these cultural threads into its sparkle, Strictly ensures it remains more than just entertainment - it becomes part of the national conversation.

The **fan experience** plays a big role too. Strictly has expanded far beyond Saturday nights. Spin-offs like *It Takes Two* give superfans their midweek fix, with behind-the-scenes gossip and rehearsal footage. The live tours, DVDs, merchandise, and social media content keep the glitterball spinning all year round. Fans don't just watch Strictly - they live it, share it, and build communities around it. By feeding this appetite for more, the show extends its relevance beyond its core broadcast slot.

Strictly also isn't afraid of **controlled experimentation.** The Couple's Choice category, allowing pros and celebs to break free from traditional styles, has been both controversial and groundbreaking. Some fans complain it's too vague, others celebrate the freedom it gives contestants to tell personal stories. But either way, it sparks debate - and debate is fuel for longevity. The producers know not every experiment will please everyone, but they also know that shaking up the formula keeps the show in the headlines.

At the same time, Strictly never loses sight of its **tradition.** The Blackpool episode remains sacred. The glitterball trophy hasn't changed. The opening theme tune still triggers a Pavlovian rush of excitement. The balance between change and continuity is what keeps Strictly fresh: enough newness to surprise, enough familiarity to comfort. It's the same reason fans return to it every autumn. No matter what's happening in the wider world, Strictly promises sequins, sparkle, and a couple of hours of joy.

There's also a deeper truth: Strictly reinvents itself because the **human stories** are always new. Each year brings a fresh cast of nervous novices, fiery pros, blossoming friendships, and unexpected journeys. Viewers never tire of watching ordinary-seeming celebs attempt extraordinary things. Even if the dances repeat - another tango, another samba - the personalities and partnerships ensure no two seasons are ever alike.

What's most remarkable is how Strictly manages to stay relevant in the streaming era. While many shows fight to hold viewers' attention, Strictly thrives on the ritual of live viewing. It's communal television, something families and friends gather around. In an age of binge-watching, Strictly offers something different: anticipation, suspense, the thrill of knowing the nation is watching with you in real time. That shared experience is part of what keeps it evergreen.

Ultimately, the glitterball keeps spinning because Strictly's producers understand one golden rule: the show must evolve, but never lose its heart. It can add new dances, new judges, new pros, new themes - but at its core, it's still about people learning to dance, connecting with their partners, and stepping into the spotlight with courage. That mixture of transformation, entertainment, and community is timeless.

As one former producer put it: "Strictly is like the ballroom itself. You can change the music, redecorate the hall, swap the dancers - but as long as two people step out, hold hands, and move together, the magic will always be there."

And so Strictly reinvents itself year after year, not by abandoning its roots, but by polishing them, re-sequinning them, and presenting them anew. It's a masterclass in television longevity - proof that when you mix tradition with innovation, and sprinkle it all with glitter, the show really can go on forever.

Next, we'll leave the wings and return to the heart of the ballroom - to the very dances themselves. Because while backstage magic keeps the show alive, it's the routines, week in and week out, that write Strictly's glittering story.

12

The Dances – From Waltz to Charleston, the Language of Strictly

The Ballroom Basics – Waltz, Foxtrot & Quickstep

S trictly is a show built on characters, costumes, and chemistry, but at its core, it is still about dancing. And the most enduring styles - the ones that have held audiences in thrall since the show began - are the ballroom classics. Waltz, foxtrot, quickstep: they are the spine of the competition, the dances that test elegance, grace, posture, and trust. They are also, in many ways, the hardest for celebrities to master, precisely because their simplicity leaves nowhere to hide.

Let's start with the **waltz**, often a contestant's first introduction to ballroom. It looks deceptively simple: slow, sweeping steps, smooth turns, and that famous rise and fall. But behind the grace lies technical precision. The waltz demands immaculate posture, perfect frame, and a deep connection between partners.

For many celebs, the hardest part isn't the steps – it's letting go of stiffness, learning to breathe into the movement, and trusting the pro to guide them across the floor. The result, when done right, is magic. Think of Jill Halfpenny's first waltz in Series Two – a revelation that ballroom could be tender, moving, and spine-tingling. Or more recently, Rose Ayling-Ellis, who brought poise and presence to a waltz that left the judges misty-eyed. The waltz is Strictly's heartbeat: pure, timeless, and emotional.

Then comes the **foxtrot,** a deceptively tricky beast. Len Good-man, the old master himself, used to say the foxtrot was the hardest of all the ballroom dances to get right. Smooth, continuous movement is the key – no jerks, no pauses, just gliding flow. It's about control, about making the difficult look effortless. Celebs often struggle with its technical demands: keeping in hold, maintaining swing and sway, and resisting the temptation to stomp through it. But when it clicks, it's glorious. Tom Chambers, the 2008 champion, is often cited for his foxtrot – suave, smooth, brimming with old-Hollywood charm. Watching a foxtrot done well is like stepping into a Fred Astaire movie, complete with tails and top hats. It harks back to ballroom's golden age, and audiences love it for that nostalgia.

And then there's the **quickstep,** the ballroom dance that separates the dabblers from the die-hards. It's fast, it's furious, and it's technically relentless. The quickstep requires stamina as much as skill, a breathless sprint across the floor filled with hops, skips, and runs. Celebs who thought they were fit quickly discover the quickstep's merciless nature. Rehearsals leave them gasping, legs aching, and tempers frayed. Yet on show night, the quickstep is a crowd-pleaser like no other. Its joy is infectious. When done well, it's impossible to watch without smiling. Harry Judd's 2011 quickstep remains a fan favourite, full of bounce and musicality. It showed how precision and energy, when balanced, can create something unforgettable.

What unites these ballroom basics is their ability to **reveal character.** Latin dances dazzle with drama and showmanship, but ballroom strips contestants bare. In hold, there's no room for ego. Celebs must submit to the discipline of the dance, the connection with their partner, and the etiquette of formality. Viewers at home pick up on this instantly. A stiff waltz feels cold. A clunky foxtrot feels awkward. But a fluid quickstep, or a romantic waltz, melts hearts. These dances showcase growth more than any other: week one waltzes often look nervous, but by the semi-finals, the same celeb can glide with newfound confidence. It's transformation in action.

The **aesthetics of ballroom** play their part too. The costumes are elegant - flowing gowns, sharp suits, tailcoats. The lighting is soft, often golden, designed to enhance the romance. The music tends toward classics, though Strictly has been known to slip in a contemporary ballad or quirky arrangement. Together, these elements create an atmosphere where ballroom feels like stepping into another world - timeless, graceful, and a little bit magical.

There are also cultural echoes at play. Ballroom is rooted in tradition, in a Britain that remembers tea dances and dance halls. For older viewers, these dances are a reminder of a bygone era. For younger ones, they're something exotic and fascinating, a window into history. This dual appeal is part of Strictly's magic: it makes the old feel new again, and the new feel timeless.

The training stories behind these dances often add to the drama. Celebs come into rehearsals convinced ballroom will be easy - slow, steady, less "embarrassing" than the Latin routines. They soon discover otherwise. Pros drill posture and frame relentlessly, often resorting to props like canes or balloons to keep elbows up. One contestant recalled being made to dance with a broom handle behind their back for hours until their shoulders stayed in place. Another described the mortification of being told, week after week, "You look like you're walking to Tesco, not dancing a foxtrot." But when the breakthrough comes - when a celeb finally learns to float instead of stomp - the sense of achievement is unmatched.

Ballroom also reveals the **emotional journeys** of contestants. A stiff politician melting into a graceful waltz, an athlete discovering the vulnerability of foxtrot, a comedian showing unexpected elegance in quickstep - these moments stick in viewers' minds. They're proof that Strictly isn't just about learning steps. It's about transformation, about people dis-covering sides of themselves they never knew existed.

Case studies abound. Joe McFadden, who many saw as the un-derdog of 2017, stunned audiences with his quickstep, proving his charm and stamina could carry him to the glitterball. Alesha Dixon, initially known for her Latin fire, wowed with a foxtrot that silenced doubters and cemented her as a true all-rounder. And Louis Smith, the gymnast, brought surprising softness to his ballroom routines, showing that elegance isn't limited to actors or singers. These stories remind us why Strictly works: the dances are mirrors, reflecting the growth, courage, and heart of each contestant.

Perhaps most importantly, ballroom basics lay the groundwork for everything else. A celebrity who masters hold, frame, and posture in waltz, foxtrot, and quickstep will find Latin dances easier, lifts more natural, and storytelling more convincing. They are the grammar of the Strictly language, the foundation upon which every glittering sentence of choreography is built.

And so, while they may not always grab the headlines, the ballroom basics are essential. They remind us of dance's timeless beauty, they reveal character, and they deliver some of the show's most moving, memorable moments. In the waltz, foxtrot, and quickstep, Strictly shows us not just how to dance, but how to grow.

Next, we'll swap elegance for heat, heading into the fiery world of Latin dance - where hips don't lie, passion rules, and the routines are as explosive as the costumes.

Latin Fire - Cha-Cha, Samba & Salsa

If ballroom is about elegance and grace, Latin is about fire and flair. These are the dances that grab you by the collar, demand your attention, and fill the Strictly floor with energy, drama, and sometimes just a little bit of chaos. The cha-cha, samba, and salsa aren't just routines - they're battles of confidence, stamina, and sheer personality. They're also the dances where the difference between natural rhythm and awkward hesitation is laid bare for the nation to see.

Let's begin with the **cha-cha,** a Strictly staple that often appears in week one. On paper, it's one of the simpler Latin styles: sharp hip action, clean lines, cheeky attitude. But in practice, it's a minefield for beginners. The cha-cha is unforgiving - it demands straight legs, precise timing, and a natural sense of rhythm. A celebrity who can't find the beat is exposed within seconds. And yet, when it works, it's electric. Denise Lewis's cha-cha in Series Two was an early template for how a celeb could balance athleticism with sass. Caroline Flack, meanwhile, used the cha-cha to cement her reputation as a Latin queen, oozing charisma while hitting every beat. For celebs, the cha-cha is less about steps and more about attitude: if you don't sell it, the judges won't buy it.

Then there's the **samba,** widely regarded as the "dance of death" among Strictly contestants. Even seasoned pros admit it's a nightmare to teach in a single week. The samba is technically one of the hardest Latin dances, built on bounce action that feels unnatural to most beginners. Add to that the stamina required to survive a full minute of relentless steps, and you've got a recipe for disaster. Yet the samba, when conquered, can be a triumph. Think of Danny Mac's samba in 2016, a performance so slick and powerful it earned a standing ovation and near-perfect scores. Or take Jill Halfpenny, whose samba remains etched in Strictly history as a routine that balanced technical brilliance with joyous freedom. The samba is a test of grit: celebs dread it, audiences love it, and judges relish the chance to see who sinks and who swims.

Finally, the **salsa** - perhaps the most unpredictable of all the Latin dances. Unlike the tightly structured cha-cha or samba, salsa thrives on lifts, tricks, and improvisation. It's the dance that shows off showmanship as much as technique. Celebs who may lack polish can still win the crowd with daring lifts and playful energy. Take Lisa Riley in 2012: her salsa was pure joy, full of cheeky grins and fearless commitment, proving entertainment value can outshine technical flaws. On the other hand, celebs who take risks with salsa can crash spectacularly. A mistimed lift or a slip in grip has the potential to create Strictly headlines for all the wrong reasons. That unpredictability is part of its appeal: you never quite know what you're going to get.

What ties these Latin dances together is their demand for **confidence.** Unlike ballroom, where posture and precision can sometimes mask nerves, Latin requires full-body commitment. Hips must move, shoulders must roll, eyes must engage with the audience. Hesitation is fatal. The cha-cha exposes stiffness, the samba punishes lack of stamina, and the salsa magnifies fear of performance. Contestants often describe feeling more vulnerable in Latin because there's nowhere to hide. You can't fake rhythm. You either have it - or you have to find it, fast.

The **training rooms** tell their own stories. Pros drill cha-cha technique relentlessly: "Straighten your legs! Push your hips! Smile!" Samba rehearsals are sweat-fests, with celebs gasping for breath halfway through run-throughs. Salsa sessions are filled with bruises from dropped lifts, laughter at failed spins, and sheer terror at the thought of throwing yourself upside down on live TV. The pros often say Latin weeks test not just their celeb's skills, but their own creativity and patience. It's one thing to train a newsreader for a waltz; it's another to coax them into hip action convincing enough for a samba.

The **costumes** for Latin dances add another layer. Ballroom gowns sweep elegantly across the floor, but Latin costumes are all about skin, sequins, and sass. Fringe is a samba essential - the faster you shake, the better it looks. Cha-cha outfits are usually bold, flirtatious, and revealing, designed to draw attention to hips and legs. Salsa costumes often border on the outrageous, giving maximum freedom for movement and maximum spectacle for the audience. For many celebs, stepping into their Latin outfit is as intimidating as the dance itself. Suddenly, they're exposed - literally and metaphorically. But that's the point. Latin dances are about shedding inhibition and embracing showbiz.

Audience reaction plays a huge part in how these dances land. A well-executed waltz may earn polite applause, but a fiery samba or cheeky salsa gets whoops, cheers, and standing ovations. Viewers respond viscerally to Latin energy, and celebs feed off that buzz. It's why some contestants become Strictly legends through their Latin routines alone. Caroline Flack, Ashley Roberts, and Kelvin Fletcher all cemented their reputations through show-stopping cha-chas and sambas that combined technique with star power.

The judges, too, treat Latin differently. Craig will savage a stiff cha-cha hip or a flat-footed samba, while Shirley delights in breaking down technical detail like bounce action or arm placement. Bruno, of course, leaps from his chair to celebrate salsa lifts, while Motsi champions the sheer joy of movement. Their reactions often mirror the audience's, creating an atmosphere where Latin nights feel louder, bolder, and riskier than ballroom weeks.

There are, of course, infamous Latin disasters. The samba has felled many a contestant, leaving them red-faced and exhausted. The cha-cha has been nicknamed the "dance of doom" in early weeks, exposing celebs before they've found their footing. And salsa lifts gone wrong are replayed endlessly on social media. Yet even the failures have value. Strictly fans love a trier, and sometimes a messy salsa can endear a celeb to the public more than a polished foxtrot ever could.

Latin dances also highlight the **cultural diversity** of Strictly. These styles are rooted in traditions from Cuba, Brazil, and the wider Latin American world. While the show presents them through a lens of Saturday-night entertainment, it also introduces millions of viewers to rhythms, movements, and histories they might never otherwise encounter. That exposure matters. It broadens horizons, adds richness to the programme, and ensures Strictly isn't just a museum of ballroom but a celebration of global dance culture.

Case studies show how transformative Latin can be. Abbey Clancy, who started Strictly with nerves, found her confidence through a sensual rumba and fiery samba, ultimately carrying her to the glitterball. Jay McGuiness, shy and reserved, shocked the nation with a salsa so slick it went viral. And Rose Ayling-Ellis's Couple's Choice dance incorporated Latin-inspired styling while breaking new ground in accessibility, showing how Latin passion could intersect with powerful storytelling.

In the end, the cha-cha, samba, and salsa are more than just dances. They are tests of courage, confidence, and stamina. They separate the entertainers from the technicians, the triers from the naturals. They give us moments of hilarity, moments of brilliance, and moments that live forever in Strictly history. Above all, they remind us why we love the show: because it's not about perfection, it's about passion.

Next, we'll explore the dances that defy easy categorisation – the quirky, theatrical, and often unexpected routines that give Strictly its unique flavour.

The Showstoppers – Charleston, Jive & Couple's Choice

Strictly has its roots in tradition, but part of its enduring charm is its willingness to embrace the playful, the theatrical, and the downright unexpected. Enter the showstoppers: the Charleston, the jive, and the controversial but game-changing Couple's Choice. These dances aren't about quiet elegance or subtle artistry. They're about making the audience roar, about throwing everything at the screen, about taking risks that either soar or stumble spectacularly. They are Strictly at its most audacious, and they're often the routines that people talk about for years.

Let's begin with the **Charleston**, a relative newcomer to Strictly's repertoire but now one of its most iconic. Rooted in the jazz age of the 1920s, the Charleston is all about energy, character, and comedy. The swivel steps, the exaggerated facial expressions, the slapstick lifts – it's a dance that demands total commitment. Celebrities who might wilt in a waltz often come alive in a Charleston, liberated by the silliness of it all. Take Chris Hollins and Ola Jordan's Charleston in 2009, which turned the underdog sports presenter into a genuine contender. Or Sophie Ellis-Bextor, whose kooky, angular style made her Charleston unforgettable. It's also the dance that helped Ore Oduba secure his glitterball - his Charleston was so sharp, so joyous, that it brought the house down. The Charleston rewards personality as much as technique, making it one of Strictly's great levellers.

Then we have the **jive**, often nicknamed the "killer" dance. Fast, furious, and physically demanding, the jive requires stamina levels bordering on superhuman. Kicks, flicks, and spins come thick and fast, testing coordination and endurance in equal measure. The jive is notorious for exposing celebs who aren't fit enough to keep up. Yet when it lands, it creates some of Strictly's most exhilarating moments. Jay McGuiness's jive to "Runaway Baby" is still hailed as one of the greatest routines in Strictly history, blending precision with effortless cool. Jill Halfpenny's jive in 2004 set the bar so high it remains legendary to this day. The jive is a Strictly rite of passage - terrifying to train, exhausting to perform, but utterly thrilling to watch.

And then there's **Couple's Choice,** Strictly's most divisive addition. Introduced in 2018, it gives celebs and pros a chance to break free from the traditional ballroom and Latin categories, exploring styles like contemporary, street/commercial, and theatre/jazz. For purists, it's a dilution of the show's ballroom roots. For others, it's a breath of fresh air that has produced some of Strictly's most powerful storytelling. Rose Ayling-Ellis and Giovanni Pernice's Couple's Choice, featuring a moment of silence to represent Rose's experience of deafness, remains one of the most moving dances ever broadcast on British television. It wasn't just dance - it was art, advocacy, and emotion all in one. Similarly, Ashley Roberts's Couple's Choice stunned with its athleticism, while Bill Bailey used his to bring quirky humour to the floor.

What unites these three showstoppers is their emphasis on **performance and individuality.** The Charleston invites celebs to ham it up, the jive pushes them to their physical limits, and Couple's Choice allows them to tell personal stories. These are the dances where celebs step outside their comfort zones, not just technically but emotionally. They're also the routines that often go viral – shared across social media, rewatched on YouTube, embedded into Strictly's cultural memory.

The **training journeys** behind these dances are often the most dramatic. Charleston rehearsals are filled with laughter, bruises from slapstick lifts, and endless reminders from pros to "SWIVEL YOUR FEET!" Jive rehearsals are brutal fitness tests, leaving celebs breathless and sore after just a few minutes of practice. Couple's Choice rehearsals can be emotionally charged, with pros drawing out personal stories from celebs, sometimes leading to tears, sometimes to breakthroughs in confidence. These dances demand not just skill but vulnerability – the willingness to throw yourself into something completely new.

The **costuming and staging** for showstoppers also stand apart. Charlestons often feature flapper dresses, braces, and bowler hats, with elaborate props to set the scene. Jives are bright, colourful, and often tied to upbeat pop hits, with costumes designed to maximise energy. Couple's Choice is the wildcard: its staging can be minimalist and raw, or spectacular and theatrical, depending on the story being told. It's the one style where pros often push the boundaries of what Strictly can look like, experimenting with lighting, props, and unconventional choices.

Audience reaction is central to the success of showstoppers. A Charleston that lands will have the crowd whooping with laughter and delight. A jive that crackles with energy brings people to their feet. A Couple's Choice that tells a powerful story can reduce the studio to tears and leave viewers at home sobbing on their sofas. These are the moments that remind everyone why they love Strictly: because it's not just entertainment, it's emotional, communal, and unforgettable.

The **judges** treat these dances with particular weight. Craig delights in dissecting the technical swivel of a Charleston or the retraction of a jive kick. Shirley offers forensic detail, particularly on Couple's Choice routines that push technique into new spaces. Bruno, unsurprisingly, goes wild for the theatricality of it all, often unable to stay in his chair. Motsi emphasises joy and connection, reminding celebs that performance value is as vital as technical accuracy. The debates they spark - over whether Couple's Choice "belongs" in the competition, or whether a Charleston deserves a ten despite sloppy technique - fuel the fan conversations that keep Strictly alive between episodes.

Of course, showstoppers can also deliver Strictly's most infamous disasters. A Charleston without swivel is painful to watch, as is a jive without energy. Couple's Choice, when it misfires, can feel indulgent or confusing. Yet even these failures are part of the fun. Fans remember them, laugh about them, debate them - they become part of the Strictly story just as much as the triumphs.

Case studies show how transformative these dances can be. Ore Oduba's Charleston turned him from an underdog into a front runner. Jay McGuiness's jive made him a Strictly legend. Rose Ayling-Ellis's Couple's Choice transcended the show entirely, becoming a cultural touchstone about representation and empathy. These routines prove that showstoppers aren't just filler weeks; they're the heart of Strictly's emotional and theatrical impact.

In the end, the Charleston, jive, and Couple's Choice remind us that Strictly is as much about storytelling and entertainment as it is about dance technique. They break the mould, defy expectations, and keep the glitterball spinning in new directions. They're the dances that turn celebs into stars, pros into innovators, and viewers into superfans.

As we leave the dances behind, we turn now to the glitterball itself - not just as a trophy, but as a symbol of everything Strictly stands for. In the next chapter, we'll explore what winning really means, how it changes careers, and why that sparkling sphere of sequins holds such power.

13

The Glitterball Dream – The Prize That Sparkles Beyond the Ballroom

The Glitterball Dream – What Winning Really Means

Every Saturday night, the sequins shimmer, the lights dazzle, and the music swells, but beneath all the sparkle lies a single, unifying goal: the glitterball trophy. It is, in the literal sense, just a mirrored sphere on a plinth - lighter than you'd imagine, a little wobbly if you touch it, a prop rather than a precious metal. Yet to the celebrities and pros who give their hearts to Strictly, it becomes something more. It's a symbol of achievement, transformation, and belonging. Winning the glitterball is not just about topping a scoreboard; it's about becoming part of a tradition that means something profound to millions of viewers.

The **emotional weight** of the trophy can't be overstated. For celebrities, many of whom enter the competition riddled with self-doubt, lifting the glitterball represents a triumph over fear.

They start the journey as amateurs - sometimes mocked for their lack of rhythm, sometimes terrified of the spotlight - and through weeks of sweat, bruises, and rehearsals, they prove to themselves, and to the nation, that they can dance. For someone like Darren Gough, the cricketer who won the very first Strictly series, the victory wasn't just about dance. It was about redefining how the public saw him: not just a sportsman, but a showman. For Bill Bailey, whose 2020 win shocked many, it was about proving that humour, musicality, and determination could triumph over youth and polish.

The **journey to the glitterball** is part of what makes the trophy so meaningful. Contestants are not judged solely on skill, but on growth. Strictly winners are rarely the best technical dancers from week one. Instead, they're the ones who connect with the public, who show vulnerability, who improve visibly and emotionally before our eyes. Alesha Dixon's win in 2007 came after she blossomed from a pop star with shaky technique into a dancer brimming with confidence and artistry. Ore Oduba's 2016 victory was about joy - a man who started out as a nervous broadcaster and ended as a natural performer. In that sense, the glitterball doesn't just reward dance talent; it rewards humanity, resilience, and relatability.

For the professionals, the glitterball is both career-defining and deeply personal. Pros invest as much, if not more, than their celebrity partners. They choreograph, train, encourage, and sometimes carry contestants through meltdowns and injuries. Winning validates their creative vision and secures their legacy on the show. Think of Oti Mabuse, whose consecutive wins with Kelvin Fletcher and Bill Bailey cemented her reputation as one of Strictly's greatest pros. Or Aljaž Škorjanec, whose glitterball triumph with Abbey Clancy remains one of the most elegant partnerships in the show's history. For pros, the trophy isn't just hardware; it's a marker of the chemistry they built, the risks they took, and the artistry they delivered.

The glitterball also has a **symbolic power** beyond the competition. For the public, it's a beacon of joy. At a time of year when nights draw in and the news cycle can be grim, Strictly offers light, laughter, and the promise of transformation. The glitterball becomes a national icon, something everyone recognises. Children mimic it in living rooms with tinfoil balls; office sweepstakes revolve around who will lift it. Winning the trophy means being etched into the cultural memory of Britain - not just as a celebrity, but as part of the Strictly family.

It's also worth noting the **career impact.** For some celebs, winning Strictly relaunches their public profile. Tom Chambers went on to star in major West End productions. Alesha Dixon transitioned from pop star to television royalty, even joining the Strictly judging panel. Stacey Dooley, after winning in 2018, expanded her broadcasting career and even found lasting love with her pro partner, Kevin Clifton. While not every winner's career skyrockets, the glitterball often opens doors, proving that the show isn't just entertainment - it's a platform.

The glitterball is also about **shared victory.** Strictly winners often speak about the friendships and bonds forged during the competition. They don't lift the trophy alone; they lift it alongside their pro partner, their fellow contestants, and even the wider backstage team. For celebs, who may have entered the competition feeling isolated, the glitterball represents community. It's a reminder that, while they danced solo under the spotlight, they were carried to victory by a team of choreographers, producers, costumers, and band members.

And then there's the **audience connection.** Viewers play a direct role in who wins the trophy. Unlike other competitions decided solely by judges, Strictly's outcome is shaped by the public vote. That means the glitterball isn't just awarded; it's bestowed by the nation. The winners are chosen by millions of people who've followed their journey, rooted for them, and felt invested in their growth. This democratic element makes the trophy even more meaningful – it's not just recognition from experts, but from ordinary people. It says: we saw you, we believed in you, we lifted you up.

The glitterball also carries an element of **legacy.** Past winners often return to perform or to cheer on new contestants, forming a kind of glittering alumni. There's a sense of continuity, of being part of a club that grows with each series. And fans remember. Even years later, names like Jill Halfpenny, Harry Judd, and Caroline Flack are recalled with warmth, their glitterball victories etched in collective memory. The trophy isn't just for one night; it's for eternity, in the scrapbook of British pop culture.

But perhaps what makes the glitterball most special is that it stands for something universal: the idea that transformation is possible. We watch Strictly not just to see celebrities dance, but to witness people step outside their comfort zones and discover something new within themselves. The glitterball embodies that possibility – that with courage, effort, and sparkle, you can do things you never imagined. That's why fans cheer so passionately, why tears flow when the winner is announced, why the glitterball still matters two decades on.

It's easy to be cynical and say "it's just a trophy." But Strictly's glitterball is more than mirrored glass. It's dreams realised, fears conquered, friendships forged, and a nation united in joy. It's proof that, sometimes, the sparkliest things in life are also the most meaningful.

And as the winners hoist it above their heads, confetti raining down, the band swelling into "We Are Family," the glitterball shines not just for them, but for all of us - reminding us that in the darkest months of the year, light, laughter, and a little bit of glitter can carry us through.

Next, we'll explore the partnerships that make the glitterball possible - those special celeb-pro pairings whose chemistry, humour, and teamwork are just as important as the steps they perform.

Partnerships That Sparkle – Celebrity & Pro Chemistry

If the glitterball is the prize, the partnerships are the journey. Strictly has always been about more than steps and scores - it's about the chemistry between celebrities and professional dancers. This chemistry is not easily defined; it's a mix of trust, humour, conflict, and connection. Some partnerships sparkle instantly, some take time to ignite, and some never quite click. But when they do, when a pro and celeb find that elusive rhythm together, the result can be pure Strictly gold.

The **celebrity-pro partnership** is unique in the world of entertainment. Where else do you take a famous face, pluck them out of their comfort zone, and hand them over to a world-class professional whose reputation depends on their success? It's a recipe for drama and triumph in equal measure. The pro has to be coach, choreographer, motivator, therapist, and sometimes friend or disciplinarian. The celebrity has to surrender ego, embrace vulnerability, and place their trust in someone they've just met. It's a dynamic that reveals character as much as choreography.

One of the most famous examples of partnership chemistry is **Abbey Clancy and Aljaž Škorjanec**. From the moment they stepped onto the floor, they had a natural rapport. Aljaž brought out Abbey's elegance, while she gave his choreography glamour and vulnerability. Their chemistry carried them all the way to the glitterball, with fans swooning over their connection. Similarly, **Stacey Dooley and Kevin Clifton** proved how partnership could blossom into something more - their rehearsals were filled with laughter, their routines full of trust, and eventually, their connection blossomed into a real-life romance.

But it's not always romantic chemistry that shines. Sometimes it's **comic partnerships** that capture the public's imagination. Think of Chris Hollins and Ola Jordan, whose banter was as entertaining as their routines. Or Ed Balls and Katya Jones, who leaned into the humour of their pairing, producing a salsa that went viral for its sheer joy. In these cases, chemistry wasn't about sexual tension or even technical brilliance - it was about connection, trust, and the courage to make fools of themselves together.

The **training room** is where partnerships are forged. Hours spent sweating, stumbling, and sometimes snapping at one another create bonds like no other. Contestants often say that their pro becomes the most important person in their life for those three months, seeing them at their best and worst. Arguments happen – exhaustion, pressure, and perfectionism can cause tempers to flare. But often, those moments of tension make the breakthroughs even sweeter. When a celeb finally nails a step after days of frustration, the joy on both faces is undeniable.

Trust is the cornerstone of these relationships. Imagine being asked to leap backwards into your partner's arms on live television, or to be spun upside down in a lift you've only mastered hours before. Without trust, it's impossible. For celebs unused to physical closeness, the intimacy of dance can be overwhelming. They must learn to let go, to be guided, to give themselves fully to the movement. When they do, something special happens: the partnership becomes greater than the sum of its parts.

The **public's perception** of partnerships is crucial too. Viewers quickly latch onto pairings they love. Social media buzzes with nicknames, fan accounts, and debates about who has "the best chemistry." Sometimes this chemistry is genuine, sometimes it's a carefully crafted narrative encouraged by producers, but either way, it fuels the Strictly story. Partnerships become characters in the wider drama: the fiery duo, the odd couple, the underdogs. Audiences don't just vote for individuals; they vote for partnerships.

It's important to note that not every partnership works. Sometimes personalities clash, or trust never fully develops.

Celebs can feel overwhelmed by strict pros; pros can become frustrated with celebs who don't commit. These mismatches often show on the dancefloor - routines feel awkward, the storytelling falls flat. And yet, even these less successful pairings contribute to the tapestry of Strictly. Not every duo can be a glitterball-winning team, but every duo adds drama, humour, or humanity to the mix.

Case studies highlight just how pivotal partnerships can be. **Jay McGuiness and Aliona Vilani** were famously understated, their quiet, low-key bond in contrast to the show's usual theatrics. Yet their trust and mutual respect culminated in Jay's legendary jive and a glitterball victory. **Rose Ayling-Ellis and Giovanni Pernice** became one of the show's most celebrated partnerships, blending Giovanni's fiery discipline with Rose's grace and resilience. Their connection transcended dance, creating a cultural moment that resonated far beyond the ballroom.

For pros, partnerships shape their own stories too. A pro who connects deeply with a celeb can become a fan favourite. Aljaž's warmth, Oti Mabuse's creative brilliance, Anton du Beke's patience with weaker dancers - these reputations were built on the partnerships they nurtured. Conversely, pros who clash with celebs can face criticism, their teaching methods scrutinised by fans and media alike. In this way, Strictly's partnerships are not just about celebs learning to dance, but about pros learning to adapt, innovate, and sometimes reinvent themselves.

Partnerships also reveal something profound about human connection. In a world where celebrities are often elevated and untouchable, Strictly strips them down to basics. Suddenly, they're sweaty, frustrated, vulnerable, relying on someone else to guide them. That vulnerability, when shared with a partner, creates bonds that are deeply relatable to audiences. We see trust being built, barriers being broken, friendships being forged. It's human drama at its most intimate, played out through sequins and sambas.

At its best, the celebrity-pro partnership becomes a kind of **alchemy.** It transforms two individuals into something magical. The celebrity brings their personality, story, and journey; the pro brings skill, creativity, and discipline. Together, they create routines that capture hearts and sometimes even change lives. That alchemy is the essence of Strictly. Without it, the glitterball would lose its meaning.

And so, while the trophy may be the destination, it's the partnerships that provide the heart of the journey. They're why viewers cry, laugh, cheer, and vote. They're why Strictly has lasted so long - because it reminds us that connection, trust, and shared joy can turn even the most unlikely pairing into something beautiful.

Next, we'll look at what happens after the confetti falls - the legacy of Strictly winners and how lifting the glitterball can reshape lives, careers, and even the show itself.

Life After Glitter - The Legacy of Strictly Winners

The moment the glitterball is lifted is unforgettable: tears flow, judges clap, the audience roars, and a celebrity and pro stand beaming under a shower of confetti. But what happens next? Life after Strictly is rarely the same as life before it. The legacy of a Strictly win – or even just a strong run in the competition – can transform careers, cement reputations, and, in some cases, change the very direction of the show itself. The glitterball, it turns out, doesn't just sparkle on Saturday night; it continues to shine for years to come.

For many winners, the glitterball becomes a **career relaunch.** A celebrity who may have been fading from the spotlight often finds themselves back in demand. Take Darren Gough, the cricketer who won the first series. His victory helped redefine him in the public eye, not just as an athlete but as a personality, paving the way for a successful broadcasting career. Alesha Dixon's win was even more transformative. Once seen primarily as a member of Mis-Teeq, her Strictly triumph propelled her into a new phase as a beloved TV personality and eventually a judge on Britain's Got Talent. The glitterball can take someone typecast in one field and give them a brand-new platform.

But the legacy isn't only professional. For many winners, Strictly has a **deep personal impact.** The journey is gruelling, vulnerable, and transformative, and lifting the trophy represents triumph over self-doubt. Stacey Dooley has spoken openly about how the experience gave her confidence and resilience, qualities she carried into her documentary career. Bill Bailey described his 2020 win as one of the proudest achievements of his life, proof that even in middle age, reinvention and growth are possible. The glitterball, for these winners, becomes a symbol not just of entertainment success but of personal transformation.

The professionals, too, feel the aftershocks. A pro's reputation can change dramatically after a glitterball win. Oti Mabuse, who lifted the trophy twice in consecutive years, cemented her place as one of Strictly's greatest pros and expanded her career into judging and television presenting. Kevin Clifton's victory with Stacey Dooley not only confirmed his skill but led to a lasting relationship that reshaped his personal life. Winning validates a pro's creative vision, strengthens their fanbase, and often ensures their place in the show's long-term legacy.

It's not just the winners who leave a mark. Some runners-up, or even contestants eliminated early, achieve remarkable post-Strictly success. Take Ed Balls, whose unforgettable "Gangnam Style" salsa turned him from a former politician into a beloved national treasure, leading to a new career in broadcasting. Or Caroline Flack, whose 2014 glitterball victory was a springboard to becoming one of the most recognisable presenters on British television. Strictly has a way of rebranding celebrities, softening their public image, or reminding audiences why they loved them in the first place.

There's also the **fan legacy.** Winners are remembered not just for their technical skill, but for their journeys. Jill Halfpenny's jive remains etched in Strictly history as the benchmark for brilliance. Harry Judd's precision, Caroline Flack's charisma, Rose Ayling-Ellis's groundbreaking performances - these moments are replayed, referenced, and celebrated by fans long after the series ends. Winning the glitterball isn't just about one night of glory; it's about securing a place in Strictly folklore, where routines are rewatched on YouTube and discussed in fan forums for years.

The legacy can also bring **pressure.** Winners often face heightened scrutiny. Can they maintain their newfound fame? Will their careers sustain the momentum? Some thrive; others struggle to live up to expectations. For pros, back-to-back wins can bring their own challenges, raising questions about favouritism or creative burnout. The glitterball shines brightly, but it can also cast long shadows.

Another important aspect of life after glitter is the **impact on the show itself.** Certain winners change the direction of Strictly. Rose Ayling-Ellis's win with Giovanni Pernice was a watershed moment, proving the power of inclusivity and accessibility. It wasn't just a personal triumph; it influenced how the show approached diversity and representation in future series. Similarly, Bill Bailey's victory demonstrated that Strictly's appeal extends across generations, challenging assumptions about who can - and should - win. These legacies shape the future of the programme, ensuring it evolves alongside its audience.

There's also the community of **Strictly alumni.** Past winners often return for Christmas specials, anniversary shows, or live tours. They become part of the fabric of the programme, a glittering club of former champions whose names are invoked every time a new series begins. This continuity deepens the sense of legacy. Fans remember, and the show thrives on that nostalgia. When a new celeb takes to the floor, they step into a lineage of glitterball dreamers stretching back to 2004.

Case studies abound of how winners have built on their Strictly legacy. Ore Oduba parlayed his victory into a successful stage career, starring in West End musicals. Louis Smith, already an Olympic hero, cemented his place as a national sweetheart. Abbey Clancy expanded her profile beyond modelling, embracing television and publishing. Each story is unique, but the common thread is reinvention. Strictly doesn't just crown dancers; it creates new identities.

The glitterball also has a **symbolic resonance for viewers.** It reminds us that transformation is possible at any stage of life. Watching a nervous, self-conscious celeb blossom into a confident performer gives audiences hope that they too could step outside their comfort zones. The legacy of winners is not just professional or personal; it's inspirational. They show us what can happen when courage meets opportunity, and when hard work is wrapped in sequins.

Of course, not every winner maintains a glittering path. Fame can be fickle, and some fade from the spotlight. But even those who disappear from headlines remain part of Strictly's mythology. Their routines live on in montages, retrospectives, and fan memories. Once you've lifted the glitterball, you're part of Strictly history forever.

In the end, life after glitter is about more than careers or reputations. It's about the stories that endure. The way a dance made us feel, the journeys we shared with contestants, the moments of joy, tears, and laughter. Strictly winners carry those memories with them, and fans carry them too. That's the true legacy: not just a shiny trophy, but the collective memory of transformation, triumph, and togetherness.

And so, as we close the chapter on the glitterball, we move to the wider legacy of Strictly itself. Beyond trophies and titles, what has this show meant to Britain? How has it shaped our culture, our television, and even the way we see ourselves? That's where we're heading next - into the broader story of Strictly's cultural footprint.

14

Strictly Fever – Britain's Glittering Obsession

Strictly Fever – How the Show Captured a Nation

On paper, Strictly Come Dancing shouldn't have worked. A Saturday night talent show where celebrities learn ballroom and Latin? It sounded quaint, old-fashioned, maybe even a little ridiculous in the era of reality juggernauts like Big Brother and Pop Idol. Yet, from its very first steps in 2004, Strictly captured Britain's imagination in a way few television programmes ever have. It wasn't just a hit show; it became a cultural phenomenon – one that brought families together, reignited a love of dance, and reminded us that glitter, glamour, and grace still had a place in our modern world.

The early years of Strictly coincided with a changing television landscape. Reality TV was everywhere, but most of it thrived on conflict, humiliation, or shock value. Strictly offered something different: positivity. Instead of tearing people down, it built them up. Celebrities weren't mocked for trying; they were applauded for improving. Judges could be sharp, but the tone was celebratory. It felt wholesome yet thrilling, a combination that resonated with audiences weary of cynicism. Families could watch together without embarrassment - grandparents admired the foxtrot, kids laughed at the slapstick training montages, and parents rooted for their favourites. It was, and remains, appointment viewing.

One of the reasons Strictly fever spread so quickly was its **blend of tradition and modernity.** Ballroom and Latin were hardly mainstream in the 21st century, but Strictly presented them with a modern twist. Classic dances were performed to contemporary pop songs, sequins were paired with special effects, and the show embraced theatricality without losing the integrity of the dance. Viewers who might never have set foot in a ballroom suddenly found themselves discussing heel leads, samba bounce, and Viennese waltz fleckerls over Sunday lunch. Strictly didn't just entertain - it educated, sparking a renewed interest in dance schools and social dancing across the country.

The **casting** played a huge role in the show's appeal. From the beginning, Strictly chose a mix of celebrities that ensured cross-generational interest: sports stars, soap actors, pop singers, newsreaders. Everyone could find someone to root for. Darren Gough appealed to sports fans, Natasha Kaplinsky to news followers, and Jill Halfpenny to drama lovers. Later, casting broadened further to include YouTubers, Paralympians, and politicians, reflecting the diversity of Britain itself. Strictly became more than just a TV show; it was a national conversation starter, uniting people across backgrounds and interests.

Music was another factor in Strictly's feverish appeal. The **live band** brought energy and authenticity, while clever song choices gave dances a modern twist. A paso doble to "Phantom of the Opera," a Charleston to "Doop," a jive to "Runaway Baby" - these unexpected pairings kept audiences hooked. The music made the show feel alive, unpredictable, and rooted in the shared soundtrack of popular culture.

Then there was the **sheer spectacle.** Strictly wasn't afraid of excess. Glitter, feathers, sequins - the show leaned into glamour with unapologetic joy. At a time when British TV often prided itself on grit and realism, Strictly gave us fantasy. For two hours on a Saturday night, viewers could escape into a world of ballgowns, mirrorballs, and perfect posture. It was camp, yes, but it was also aspirational. Who wouldn't want to swap the weekly supermarket run for a spin in sequins under studio lights?

The judges also played a role in fanning Strictly fever. **Len Goodman's** avuncular charm balanced Craig Revel Horwood's sharp wit. Bruno Tonioli's theatrical enthusiasm contrasted with Arlene Phillips's technical precision. Later additions like Darcey Bussell, Shirley Ballas, and Motsi Mabuse kept the panel fresh while maintaining the show's balance of critique and encouragement. Their banter became as much a part of Saturday nights as the dances themselves, spawning catchphrases ("fab-u-lous!") that entered the national lexicon.

But perhaps the most powerful factor was the **emotional journey.** Strictly wasn't just about watching celebrities dance; it was about watching them change. Viewers saw nerves transform into confidence, clumsiness into grace, doubt into joy. Every season produced stories that resonated: a widower finding joy again through dance, a young woman gaining confidence after years of insecurity, a sportsman discovering vulnerability. These narratives kept audiences invested, rooting for contestants as if they were family. Strictly fever wasn't just about entertainment; it was about empathy.

The communal aspect of Strictly cannot be overstated. In a fragmented media world, Strictly created a shared cultural space. Millions tuned in at the same time, week after week, to watch live. Social media amplified the buzz, but the show's true magic lay in its ability to get people talking offline - in schools, workplaces, and pubs. "Did you see that jive last night?" became a Monday morning refrain. Strictly wasn't just television; it was ritual, a glittery thread woven into the fabric of British weekends.

Case studies highlight the fever at its peak. Jill Halfpenny's jive in 2004 was so iconic that it's still cited as one of the best routines in Strictly history. Jay McGuiness's 2015 jive went viral, reaching audiences far beyond the UK. Rose Ayling-Ellis's Couple's Choice in 2021 made headlines worldwide for its groundbreaking use of silence. These moments transcended the show, becoming cultural landmarks. Strictly fever meant that, for a brief moment, the whole country seemed to be talking about the same thing.

The show's reach extended beyond the screen. **Strictly tours** filled arenas, bringing the magic live to thousands. Dance schools reported surges in interest after standout routines. Costume trends filtered into fashion - sequins, fringe, and feathers made their way from the Strictly floor to high street shops. Even weddings saw an influence, with couples inspired to choreograph their first dances. Strictly fever seeped into everyday life, making dance feel accessible, exciting, and relevant again.

Crucially, Strictly managed to avoid the burnout that plagues many long-running shows. Part of this resilience lies in its adaptability. It embraced theme weeks, introduced new dances like the Charleston and Couple's Choice, and refreshed its judging panel without losing its identity. Strictly fever remained because the show kept evolving while staying true to its core: the joy of dance.

The fever also reflects something deeper in the national psyche. Strictly taps into Britain's love of underdogs, transformation, and a bit of camp spectacle. It celebrates effort over perfection, courage over cynicism. It's aspirational without being elitist, glamorous without being inaccessible. At its heart, Strictly fever is about joy - the joy of movement, music, and connection. And in a world that often feels heavy, that joy is priceless.

As we look back at how Strictly fever gripped the nation, it's clear that this wasn't just about a TV show. It was about community, identity, and hope. Strictly became more than Saturday night entertainment; it became a national institution.

And so, having seen how Strictly captured Britain's heart, we now turn to its influence abroad. The format didn't just thrive here - it spread across the world, becoming a global dance sensation.

Dancing Across Borders – Strictly's Global Impact

Strictly Come Dancing was born in a BBC studio in 2004, but its story didn't end there. Almost as soon as sequins first glittered under the studio lights, the format was snapped up, rebranded, and exported to the world. Today, Strictly – or *Dancing with the Stars* as it is known in many countries – is one of the most successful television franchises in history. From New York to New Zealand, from Mumbai to Mexico City, audiences have been swept up in the same blend of glamour, grit, and glitter that first captured Britain's heart. The global impact of Strictly isn't just about TV ratings; it's about cultural exchange, international stardom, and the way dance has become a universal language of entertainment.

The franchise's expansion was swift. After the BBC struck gold with Strictly's format, international broadcasters scrambled to buy the rights. The United States was among the first, launching *Dancing with the Stars* in 2005. What many thought might be a niche curiosity became a smash hit, running for over 30 seasons and pulling in millions of viewers each week. Its American success was crucial in proving that ballroom, once seen as niche or outdated, could be made mainstream, modern, and massively popular.

The **US version** brought its own flavour. Where the British Strictly leaned into camp charm and family warmth, *Dancing with the Stars* embraced Hollywood glitz. Bigger sets, more dramatic staging, and a celebrity pool that included film stars, athletes, and even politicians gave it a distinctly American feel. Yet at its heart, it was the same show: ordinary celebrities, extraordinary transformations. Winners like Olympic gymnast Shawn Johnson and deaf model Nyle DiMarco became household names, their journeys celebrated far beyond the ballroom.

From America, the Strictly format spread across Europe, Asia, Africa, and beyond. In total, more than **60 countries** have produced their own versions. Each adaptation reflects local tastes and cultures. In **India**, *Jhalak Dikhhla Jaa* combined the Strictly format with Bollywood flair, with routines infused with traditional Indian dance styles alongside cha-chas and rumbas. In **Argentina**, *Bailando por un Sueño* added a soap-opera intensity, with storylines and drama as central to the show as the dances themselves. In **China**, *Dancing with the Stars* fused ballroom with local pop culture, creating a hybrid spectacle that attracted millions of viewers.

The success of these adaptations highlights the **universal appeal of dance.** Ballroom and Latin may originate from specific cultural traditions, but their essence - rhythm, movement, expression - transcends borders. Audiences from Brazil to Bulgaria could connect with the joy of seeing a nervous celebrity blossom into a confident performer. The story was the same everywhere: vulnerability, transformation, triumph. The glitterball, it turned out, needed no translation.

The global reach of Strictly also created opportunities for **cross-cultural exchange.** Pros who trained in one country sometimes found themselves competing in another. Dancers like Artem Chigvintsev, who started in the UK, later joined the American version, bringing with them a sense of international continuity. Some stars even competed in multiple versions - Pamela Anderson, for example, appeared on both the US and Argentinian shows. This cross-pollination strengthened the franchise, blending styles and broadening the scope of what ballroom on TV could be.

Interestingly, while the core format remained the same, cultural differences shaped the shows in subtle ways. In Britain, humour and underdog stories often resonated most – Ed Balls surviving week after week thanks to public votes is a very British phenomenon. In the US, athletic excellence and showbiz polish carried more weight, with Olympians and pop stars often dominating. In Latin America, passion and drama took centre stage, with routines spiced up by intensity and storytelling. These variations reflected national identities, but the Strictly DNA – glitter, growth, and a dash of drama – remained intact.

The **economic impact** of the franchise has been immense. Live tours, merchandise, albums of the house band's performances, and spin-off specials have all generated millions. In many countries, Strictly has revitalised interest in dance schools, with classes in cha-cha, tango, and salsa booming after standout TV routines. The format didn't just entertain; it created industries around dance, costuming, and live performance.

The franchise also fostered **moments of international cultural resonance.** In the US, Nyle DiMarco's silent section in his paso doble mirrored the impact of Rose Ayling-Ellis's Couple's Choice in the UK, showing how the format could be used to highlight issues of accessibility and representation. In Israel, same-sex pairings sparked conversations about inclusivity, paving the way for similar moves in other countries. In Ireland, *Dancing with the Stars* brought communities together in a way that echoed Strictly's unifying power in Britain. Wherever it landed, the show became a stage for broader social discussions.

The global impact of Strictly also influenced the **perception of dance professionals.** Once confined largely to competitive circuits, pros found themselves transformed into international stars. Dancers like Derek Hough in the US, Kym Johnson in Australia, and Giovanni Pernice in the UK became household names, their careers flourishing far beyond the competitive ballroom world. This elevation of professional dancers to celebrity status was one of the franchise's most radical contributions - proof that talent, charisma, and hard work could turn technicians into stars.

The global glitterball effect even extended into **politics and diplomacy.** In some countries, politicians who took part in their local version used it to soften their public image, showing humour and humanity on the dancefloor. In others, the inclusion of disabled contestants or same-sex pairings sparked national debates, pushing forward conversations about representation and equality. Strictly, exported across the world, became more than entertainment: it became cultural commentary, packaged in sequins and smiles.

Case studies show just how enduring Strictly's international appeal has been. In Australia, the show has run for over 20 seasons, creating its own glitterball legends. In Italy, *Ballando con le Stelle* is a primetime institution, blending Mediterranean passion with ballroom tradition. In South Africa, the show's diverse casting and vibrant energy has made it one of the most-watched programmes in the country. Each version leaves its own footprint, but all share the same glittering DNA.

Ultimately, Strictly's global journey proves the **power of joy.** In a fractured media landscape, it united audiences across languages and borders. Whether in London, Los Angeles, or Lagos, the thrill of a foxtrot done well, the drama of a salsa lift, or the triumph of a nervous celeb finally nailing a routine resonated the same way. Dance, after all, is universal. And Strictly, in its many incarnations, tapped into that truth better than almost any other show of the modern era.

The legacy of Strictly abroad also feeds back into the UK original. Seeing what works internationally – from daring production values to bold casting decisions – has inspired the British version to keep evolving. Conversely, the British show remains the gold standard, the parent of a glittering family of sequinned spin-offs.

And so, as Strictly fever spread across borders, it didn't just entertain millions. It reminded the world that joy, courage, and connection could unite us, no matter our backgrounds. The glitterball became a global icon, a shimmering beacon of hope and happiness.

Having seen Strictly conquer the world, we now turn back home to look at its **lasting cultural footprint in Britain.**Beyond ratings and routines, how has Strictly shaped our society, our values, and even our sense of who we are? That's where we'll step next.

Glitter in the Bloodstream – Strictly's Lasting Cultural Footprint

Strictly Come Dancing began as a television experiment, but over two decades it has become part of Britain's cultural DNA. To say it's "just a TV show" is to miss the point. Strictly has seeped into the bloodstream of the nation, influencing fashion, music, social life, and even politics. It's a programme that's managed to be both escapist fantasy and everyday reality, uniting millions in front of their screens and inspiring countless to take to the dancefloor themselves. Its lasting cultural footprint is as glittery as the confetti that rains down on finale night.

The most obvious impact has been the **revival of dance in Britain.** Before Strictly, ballroom and Latin were niche pursuits, largely confined to competitive circuits and ageing social clubs. Strictly changed that. Almost overnight, interest in local dance classes surged. Dance schools reported waiting lists for cha-cha, tango, and salsa lessons. Wedding couples began choreographing their first dances with a Strictly-inspired flair. Even children wanted in, with ballroom classes becoming as popular as football in some towns. The show didn't just put dance on television; it put it back into people's lives.

Fashion, too, felt the Strictly effect. Sequins, fringe, and feathers spilled from the studio into high street shops. The "Strictly look" - glamorous, bold, unapologetically sparkly - became a seasonal staple, particularly in the run-up to Christmas. High-street brands cashed in with "Strictly-style" collections, while costume designers from the show became minor celebrities in their own right. Suddenly, glitter wasn't tacky;

it was aspirational. Dressing like a Strictly contestant meant embracing joy, confidence, and fun.

Strictly also changed the **soundtrack of Saturday nights.** The live band's interpretations of pop hits gave viewers new appreciation for old classics and fresh spins on current chart-toppers. Songs performed on Strictly often re-entered the charts the following week. Musical guests clamoured for a slot on the results show, knowing the Strictly stage carried prestige and reach. For many families, Strictly was not just about dance but about music discovery, reminding us that live performance still had magic in an age of streaming.

The cultural footprint extended into **language and humour.** Catchphrases like Craig Revel Horwood's "a dis-as-ter, darling," Bruno Tonioli's excitable outbursts, and Len Goodman's "se-ven!" became part of everyday banter. Office conversations echoed with talk of "heel leads" and "paso faces." Even those who didn't watch could recognise the references. Strictly gave Britain a shared vocabulary of glitter and giggles, a cultural shorthand that cut across age and background.

Politically, Strictly has played a subtle but notable role. The casting of politicians - from Ann Widdecombe's comedy routines to Ed Balls's viral Gangnam Style - softened public perceptions and sparked conversations about humanity in politics. These appearances reminded viewers that even the most serious figures could be vulnerable, funny, and relatable. While some critics accused the show of trivialising politics, others saw it as a form of humanising theatre, where public figures could step out of their usual roles and connect with audiences on a personal level.

Inclusivity has been one of Strictly's most profound contributions. Over the years, the show has gradually embraced greater **diversity in casting and storytelling.** Contestants have ranged from Paralympians like Jonnie Peacock to trailblazers like Rose Ayling-Ellis, whose silent moment with Giovanni Pernice changed how Britain thought about deafness. Same-sex partnerships, once unthinkable on primetime TV, became a celebrated reality with Nicola Adams and Katya Jones, and later Johannes Radebe and John Whaite. These choices weren't just about dance; they were about shifting cultural attitudes, normalising representation, and pushing Britain towards greater inclusivity.

The cultural footprint can also be seen in the **rituals of British life.** Strictly became synonymous with autumn and winter. The dark nights drew in, the heating went on, and families gathered around the TV for the comfort of sequins and samba rolls. It became as much a part of the seasonal calendar as Bonfire Night or Christmas markets. "Strictly season" meant comfort, community, and sparkle. It gave structure to the year, a glittering countdown from September to Christmas.

At a time when many lamented the decline of shared national experiences, Strictly provided one. Millions watched the same show at the same time, week after week, in an era when streaming and on-demand viewing fractured audiences. Strictly was, and still is, one of the last great communal TV events in Britain. Its finales rivaled sporting events in viewership. Its impact was not just in numbers, but in the sense of togetherness it fostered. It reminded us of the power of gathering, laughing, crying, and voting as a community.

Strictly has also left its mark on the **next generation.** Children who grew up watching the show were inspired to dance, to perform, to pursue creative careers. Dance schools flourished, and some even produced future Strictly professionals. The programme planted seeds of aspiration, proving that dance was not an elite pursuit but an accessible, joyful form of self-expression. The glitterball wasn't just for celebrities; it was for anyone brave enough to step onto a dancefloor.

Case studies illustrate how deep this cultural footprint runs. Rose Ayling-Ellis's Couple's Choice was replayed in classrooms, used to spark discussions about accessibility and inclusion. Caroline Flack's win became a touchstone for conversations about mental health and the pressures of fame. Bill Bailey's victory gave older viewers a role model for reinvention. Strictly moments became cultural landmarks, referenced in newspapers, classrooms, and even parliamentary debates.

Even critics of the show, who sneer at its sequins or question its longevity, can't deny its influence. Strictly has changed the way Britain thinks about entertainment, inclusivity, and even itself. It has shown that joy can be powerful, that glamour can coexist with grit, and that transformation is worth celebrating. In a divided world, Strictly became a rare unifier.

Perhaps the greatest sign of its cultural footprint is how seamlessly Strictly has woven itself into the fabric of national identity. It's hard to imagine autumn Saturdays without it. It's become part of who we are: a glittery constant in a changing world. Strictly fever wasn't a passing craze; it was the start of something enduring.

And so, as we step off the floor of Strictly's cultural impact, our journey moves towards the final curtain. We've seen the roots, the stars, the drama, the dances, and the fever. Now, it's time to reflect on what Strictly means after nearly two decades: why it endures, what it teaches us, and what its future might hold.

15

The Last Dance – Why Strictly Still Sparkles

As the band strikes up its final chords and the confetti settles over the studio floor, Strictly Come Dancing remains what it has always been: a show about far more than sequins and sambas. It is, at its heart, about transformation, courage, joy, and community. After nearly two decades, the sparkle has not dimmed - if anything, it shines brighter, its legacy secure as one of Britain's most beloved cultural institutions. But why does Strictly still sparkle? Why has a show rooted in ballroom tradition, launched at a time when reality TV was dominated by cynicism, become a perennial favourite? The answers lie in its unique blend of entertainment, humanity, and hope.

The first reason is **its capacity for reinvention.** Strictly has never stood still. New dances, theme weeks, judging panels, and innovations like the Couple's Choice category have kept the show fresh. Where other reality competitions burn out after a handful of series, Strictly has adapted while staying true to its essence: celebrities learning to dance with professionals. It's a format simple enough to be timeless, flexible enough to embrace change. That balance between tradition and modernity keeps audiences coming back, year after year.

Secondly, Strictly sparkles because of its **celebration of effort over perfection.** Unlike shows that chase flawless performances, Strictly thrives on journeys. The celebrity who begins with two left feet but slowly blossoms embodies the spirit of the show. It reassures us that courage matters more than natural talent, that growth is possible at any stage of life. Watching someone like Bill Bailey master the quickstep or Rose Ayling-Ellis redefine what performance can be reminds us that transformation is within reach for all of us.

Then there's the **emotional core.** Strictly's stories connect on a human level. It isn't about fame or fortune - it's about vulnerability, trust, and joy. The rehearsals where tears fall, the moments of doubt before a live show, the exhilaration of a perfect routine - these are deeply relatable experiences, dressed in sequins. Strictly's sparkle comes not from rhinestones alone but from the way it reflects our shared humanity, showing us people at their most open and courageous.

The **community spirit** surrounding Strictly is another reason it endures. Few shows unite families quite like it. Children, parents, and grandparents can all sit down together, each finding their own favourites. It's intergenerational, inclusive, and communal in a way few television experiences are today. Even in an era of fragmented streaming, Strictly remains one of the last true national rituals - millions tuning in at the same time, sharing laughter, tears, and debates over who should have stayed or gone. In its glittery way, Strictly has kept alive the art of gathering.

The show's **cultural impact** also sustains its sparkle. It has revived interest in dance, reshaped fashion trends, influenced music charts, and broadened social attitudes. It has been a platform for inclusion, from same-sex partnerships to deaf and disabled representation. It has humanised politicians, relaunched careers, and inspired children to dance. Strictly has shown that entertainment can do more than amuse; it can educate, challenge, and shift perceptions, all while wrapped in glitter and joy.

What makes Strictly truly timeless, though, is its **message of hope.** Each series tells the same story in different costumes: that with courage, support, and hard work, transformation is possible. The celebrities' journeys mirror our own struggles with fear, self-doubt, and resilience. The glitterball becomes a metaphor for the triumphs we all strive for, however modest. Strictly sparkles because it reflects something deeply human: the desire to grow, to connect, to shine.

The personalities who've graced its stage have also become part of the show's magic. From Len Goodman's warmth to Claudia Winkleman's wit, from Craig Revel Horwood's razor-sharp critiques to Tess Daly's reassuring steadiness, Strictly has cultivated a cast of characters who feel like family. Professional dancers have risen from obscurity to become household names, embodying the show's ethos that hard work and charisma can make stars of anyone. Contestants have become legends - Jill Halfpenny's jive, Jay McGuiness's quiet brilliance, Rose Ayling-Ellis's trailblazing silence. These moments sparkle in memory, proof that Strictly's legacy is built on stories as much as steps.

The sparkle is sustained, too, by the **audience themselves.** Viewers don't just watch; they participate. Through voting, they shape the outcome, ensuring that Strictly's winners reflect not just technical skill but public connection. The glitterball belongs as much to the nation as to the dancers who lift it. This democratic element ensures the show remains rooted in the people's voice, renewing its relevance each year.

Case studies underline just how powerful this sparkle remains. Caroline Flack's win, tinged with later tragedy, reminded us of the pressures of fame and the joy the show can bring in fleeting moments. Bill Bailey's triumph offered hope and humour in the dark days of the pandemic. Rose Ayling-Ellis's routines opened a national conversation about accessibility and inclusivity. Each series delivers moments that ripple beyond the studio, moments that matter because they touch something deeper in the collective imagination.

And then there's the glamour. Let's not underestimate the simple power of sequins, feathers, and big band music. Strictly sparkles because it dares to be unapologetically joyous. In a culture that often prizes irony, Strictly embraces sincerity. It says: it's okay to cheer, to cry, to laugh, to dress up, to dance. It reminds us that joy is not frivolous but essential. That, perhaps, is the truest reason it endures.

Looking ahead, Strictly's sparkle seems set to last. New generations of viewers continue to join the glitterball family. Technological changes may shift how we watch, but the essence - celebrities learning to dance, audiences cheering them on - remains timeless. Future series may experiment with virtual reality, interactive features, or new dance styles, but the heart will remain unchanged. Strictly sparkles because it taps into something eternal: the joy of movement, the courage of vulnerability, and the magic of connection.

As the credits roll on another series, as pros and celebs hug, and as the glitterball is raised once more, Strictly reminds us of something vital. That no matter who we are, where we come from, or how many left feet we believe we have, joy is within reach. We just have to step onto the floor, take someone's hand, and dance.

That's why Strictly still sparkles. Because it is more than a show. It is a celebration of life, of resilience, of community. It is, in its glittering way, a mirrorball held up to who we are and who we aspire to be. And as long as Britain craves joy, transformation, and a little bit of sparkle on a Saturday night, Strictly will keep on shining.

16

Author's Note

Dear reader

When I first watched *Strictly Come Dancing* in 2004, I had no idea it would become such a fixture in my life. I'd already hung up my competitive shoes by then, but the show rekindled the same fire that drove me onto dancefloors around the world in my twenties. Every autumn since, I've sat down with a cup of tea, my two sausage dogs - Fred and Ginger - curled up beside me, and felt that familiar flutter as the titles rolled. It never fails to thrill.

Writing this book has been a joy because it's given me the chance to reflect on why Strictly matters so much, not just to me but to millions. The truth is, it's never been about perfect scores or immaculate technique. It's about the courage to take a risk, the laughter in the rehearsal room, the tears when things go wrong, and the roar of triumph when they finally go right. That's what makes it magic.

In my dance school, I see echoes of Strictly every week. The nervous groom learning his first steps before the big day, the pensioner rediscovering her love of movement, the child who finds confidence in a cha-cha. Strictly's greatest gift is that it reminds us dance belongs to everyone. It doesn't matter if you're an Olympic gymnast, a newsreader, or an accountant from Sussex – with a little patience, a lot of heart, and perhaps a sequin or two, anyone can feel the joy of movement.

If this book has captured even a fraction of that joy, then I've done my job. Strictly is, at its heart, a love letter – to dance, to courage, to connection. It's also a mirrorball reflecting who we are as a nation: sometimes silly, often stubborn, but always ready to celebrate when the band strikes up.

So thank you for joining me on this glittering journey. Whether you've been a fan since the first spin of the glitterball or you've only just discovered the joy of Strictly, I hope you keep dancing, keep laughing, and keep believing in the power of sparkle.

Now, if you'll excuse me, Fred and Ginger are pawing at my leg – apparently it's time for their evening waltz around the kitchen.

With sequins, sweat, and all my sparkle,

Bruce Templeton

X

Printed in Dunstable, United Kingdom